PRAISE FOR

IS YOUR WALLET KILLING YOU? FINANCIAL CPR™

In their book, *Is Your Wallet Killing You? Financial CPR*, Shumard and Ferderer, (lawyers with a conscience) reveal the truth they learned from your creditors. In fact, the information here could increase your net worth by hundreds of thousands of dollars overnight. If you're in financial crisis, don't wait another minute to read this book.

— RICHARD PAUL EVANS
NEW YORK TIMES BESTSELLING AUTHOR OF
THE 5 LESSONS A MILLIONAIRE TAUGHT ME

Hundreds of billions to bail out the banks. But what about you? *Is Your Wallet Killing You? Financial CPR* reveals what you need to know about *your* financial bailout.

— ROBERT G. ALLEN
NEW YORK TIMES BESTSELLING AUTHOR OF
NOTHING DOWN AND *CREATING WEALTH*

Is Your Wallet Killing You?

FINANCIAL CPR™
From Bankruptcy Attorneys to Save Your Financial Life

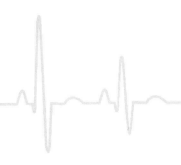

Jo Anne Shumard, J.D.
Stuart Ferderer, J.D.

BookWise
publishing

Is Your Wallet Killing You?
Financial CPR™ From Bankruptcy Attorneys to Save Your Financial Life
Jo Anne Shumard and Stuart Ferderer

BookWise Publishing
65 E. Wadsworth Park Drive, Suite 110
Draper, Utah 84020
www.bookwise.com

www.isyourwalletkillingyou.com

Book design: Eden Design, Salt Lake City, Utah

ISBN: 978-1-60645-038-3
10 9 8 7 6 5 4 3 2 1
First Printing

PRINTED IN THE UNITED STATES OF AMERICA

DISCLAIMER

The following information is not to be construed as legal advice. Consult legal counsel in your state concerning your facts and circumstances before making any decisions about your financial situation.

TO OUR READERS

WHY WE WROTE THIS BOOK

Financial issues are fused to our emotions. We are happy when we think we're rich. We are sad when we think we're poor. Similarly, we feel exhilarated when we have money in our pockets and sick when we can't pay the bills. This experience is universal to the clients we see in our office every day. They carry the weight of the world on their shoulders when they walk in and sit down.

We have seen that weight lifted after just one meeting. That *one meeting* has changed so many lives for the better that we felt it was important to bring the same gift to as many people as possible. This book is written for you—the person who may need the help we provide but who has been reluctant to seek it, for whatever reason.

As you progress through *Is Your Wallet Killing You*, we hope that you, too, will begin to feel the pressure lifting and your hope restored. Your fresh start begins now.

—Jo Anne Shumard, J.D. and Stuart Ferderer, J.D.

DEDICATION

*To our sons, Ryan and Taylor, our extended family,
and our friends who are constant reminders that net worth
has little to do with numbers on a balance sheet,
and everything to do with whom you love
and those who love you.*

ACKNOWLEDGEMENTS

We are very grateful to all who contributed to this book, in particular our clients, who inspire us and entrust their friends and relatives to our care. Many of the common experiences shared by our clients are revealed within these pages. All the names are fictitious, but the stories are true and all too common. We respectfully share their experiences with you in the hope that they will help you find your own truth. Also, we are grateful to Suzette Fine, Robert Fine, and Charles Davidson who provided their insight and resources along the way, and to Annette Lyon, Heather Moore, and Karen Christoffersen who watched over each word. Additionally, we wish to acknowledge Fran Platt's creative genius exhibited in the book cover and design.

Our legal careers have been enriched by our professional relationship with the Judges and Clerks Office in the Middle District of Florida, Orlando Division, where we practice. We are eternally grateful for the wisdom, patience, and professionalism demonstrated by all within the court system. As members of the Bankruptcy Bar in Orlando, Florida, we serve the honest and unfortunate individuals who seek the help Congress designed for them. Each city in the United States has attorneys in this specialty who dedicate their professional lives to helping others. We urge those reading this book who have questions relevant to their specific circumstances to seek out experienced attorneys who specialize in bankruptcy. They can advise you on the law in your state relevant to your specific facts and circumstances.

Finally, we thank *New York Times* bestselling authors Richard Paul Evans and Robert G. Allen for sharing their wisdom and insight. Without them, this book may have never reached your hands. We are most grateful for their generosity of spirit and their willingness to ensure that this important message is delivered to the hands of those so desperately in need of it.

CONTENTS

FOREWORD

For many years the media has provided us with experts in the financial field. These experts were usually former stockbrokers, investment bankers or financial planners. In recent years, as the economy deteriorated, these same "experts" tried to speak the language of bankruptcy. While they knew enough to carry on a basic conversation, in truth they were nothing more than visitors to a foreign land with no background in the trenches of an often misunderstood world. Tragically this didn't always stop them from giving advice, and trusting listeners were often led into a wilderness where they wandered aimlessly, unable to find their way out.

Bankruptcy is much more than numbers on a balance sheet. It is a difficult and oftentimes complex journey–emotionally and fiscally–where a family or individual navigates their way from the first symptoms of trouble and a realization that they need help, to obtaining the information they need for a fresh start. This journey requires a special guide, one who knows the way and the terrain and can steer you away from pitfalls—a guide who understands dollars and *sense*–the kind of sense that comes from real life experience.

How refreshing it is to find in this book a dynamic duo of travel guides—legal eagles who can take you on a flight far above the landscape providing not only a bird's eye view of the terrain, but also the horizon ahead. In *IS YOUR WALLET KILLING YOU?* your new guides, Shumard and Ferderer, provide you with a simple map, leaving you confident on a path that will greatly affect your life.

A wise man once said, "The truth will set you free." This book is filled with truth. Enjoy the freedom.

—RICHARD PAUL EVANS

THE WARNING SIGNS

The deadliest form of delay is denial.

— C. Northcutte Parkinson —

CHAPTER ONE

911

It was May 29, 1997. I was thirty-nine, a litigator trained by the best legal boot camp in the South. I knew how to sue, foreclose, execute on judgments, levy on personal property, garnish bank accounts, and find assets people thought they had effectively hidden. I had been a litigator in Orlando for nine years and had filed foreclosures against hundreds of people. During my training, my colleagues and I laughed when a senior partner told how he'd levied on a man's beloved pet dog to force the heartbroken owner to pay a debt. That was my training ground, and I was a star pupil.

But this night, I wasn't laughing. I returned home after a long day at work followed by a frenzied trip to McDonald's with the kids before a school recital. We scooted out as soon as the recital was over because I was desperately weak with exhaustion. As we all cozied up to our favorite evening routines, I felt an odd cramp in my left breast. It came and went so fast, I wondered if it really happened at all. A few minutes later, I felt like a horse kicked me in my chest. It was only for a second. Then—poof—it was gone. I was too young to be having a heart attack, and we were all way too tired to be dragged through a trip to the emergency room.

Another sharp cramp. It felt like a labor pain, I thought, but it was certainly in the wrong place. I said nothing. By now, forty-five minutes had passed. Another pain hit, and my vision went black. Again, it was over so quickly, I wondered if I had imagined it. About fifteen minutes later, another pain hit me, and sure enough, my vision closed down into a shrinking tunnel like the TV screen after a cartoon. This time I kept my eyes wide open to see if that would make any difference to my vision. Nope.

I couldn't deny it any longer. I had a family that relied on me. I had to do something. All the signs were there, but I hated to cause any trouble to the people I loved.

"Stuart, I hate to say this . . . but I think I'm having a heart attack," I said.

His newspaper flew into the air.

"Call the hospital and see if they take our insurance," I said. "Call the neighbors to see if they can take Taylor and Ryan. We'd better get going."

Boy, did we do a lot of things wrong. We drove to the emergency room, where I motioned for a young woman who was beaten and bleeding to go ahead of me. We waited.

An hour and a half after drawing my blood, the results came back. The ER doctor put on her glasses.

"You've had a heart attack and need to go to ICU," she said. "You're not the typical heart attack victim, but every situation is different. You have to listen to your symptoms. It's a good thing you came in when you did. Waiting could have cost you your life." They wheeled me off to ICU.

With time and rehabilitation, I recovered physically. Emotional recovery was harder. I was insulted by my heart attack. I was a vegetarian and worked out several times a week. *This never should have happened to me.*

As I recuperated, I worked in my husband's practice, meeting clients with financial problems. I remembered back when I represented creditors, being annoyed that he did *that* kind of work. I didn't get it. Then, as I started meeting with his clients, I saw that they were just like us. As I started to understand, I started to grow a heart.

And my own heart healed.

The folks who have come to see us about their financial issues remind me of my denial when I first felt chest pains. They, too, are in denial. They had so many perfectly good reasons explaining why financial crisis couldn't be happening to them. They'd made a good living for most of their professional lives. They knew how to bounce back. Things would get better; all they needed to do was take out a home equity line of credit and everything would be okay. Or they could borrow against their retirement plan. They thought they knew what to do without asking for help. Or they knew people who were surely experts on the subject.

They didn't realize just how life-threatening their mistakes were.

Bankruptcy was out of the question. They didn't know much about it and had no interest in finding out about it. Bankruptcy is immoral, they thought. Unethical. Against their religion. Against everything they ever believed in. "Only deadbeats file bankruptcies," they'd always heard.

Their financial crisis was just as life-threatening as the cardiac crisis I denied. I should have dialed 911 and called for an ambulance. I didn't and because of that choice, I could have died, leaving my young family without a mother.

But the reason I didn't call was because I didn't want to be "one of those people."

Just like me, our clients needed Financial CPR—stat—from a real expert.

Your financial crisis is a real threat to your life and to your family's well-being. Money problems know no boundaries, and everything you think you know about them is probably wrong.

Here's your prescription—read the instructions inside this book and follow them as directed. Your life and that of your family depend upon it.

CHAPTER TWO

IDENTIFY THE WARNING SIGNS

If you think nobody cares if you're alive,
try missing a couple of car payments.

— EARL WILSON —

You may be one of many who have suffered divorce, death, a job loss, a medical crisis, or some other catastrophe that put you in severe debt. Whatever the reason for your financial problems, the following questions will help determine whether you're in a financial crisis.

We ask all individuals with life partners to take this quiz separately, then trade your answers with your partner. **Be honest with yourself *and* with your partner.** That is the only way you'll be able to save your financial life.

THE TOP FIVE WARNING SIGNS
OF FINANCIAL CRISIS

1. Are you unable to pay your monthly living expenses while paying down your debt?
2. Is your debt situation causing stress and strain on your personal relationships?
3. Are you afraid to answer your phone or open your mail?
4. Have your borrowed money or are you thinking about borrowing from your retirement account to pay debts? If you don't have a retirement account, is it because all your money is going to pay debt?
5. Does your debt situation cause feelings of hopelessness and despair?

Here's the good news. Identifying the warning signs is the first step. When you know the warning signs of serious illness, just like the warning signs of a heart attack or a stroke, you can do something about it. You may have a magnet on your refrigerator that has the warning signs for heart attack and stroke. It tells you to call 911 if you have any of the symptoms.

Similarly these are the five critical warning signs of financial illness. If you answered "yes" to one or more of the top five, you are in financial crisis. Your 911 call should be to a bankruptcy specialist in your area. This does not mean you have to file bankruptcy any more than calling 911 means you're having a heart attack or stroke. However a professional needs to fully evaluate your situation and make a recommendation for you. Information is potent medicine.

There are attorneys in most communities who specialize in bankruptcy and have years of experience navigating through the

Bankruptcy Code. Those are the attorneys you are looking for—specialists in this area. The more experience they have, the better.

MORE WARNING SIGNS

- Are you unable to make either your house or car payment?
- Are you paying more than 18% interest on any of your credit card debts?
- Do you have negative cash flow on an investment property?
- Are you considering taking out a home equity loan to pay off credit cards or finance mortgage debt on investment property?
- Are you considering taking out money from the cash value of a life insurance policy or annuity to pay off debt?

If you answered "yes" to one of these questions, it is much like having been exposed to a contagious disease. Be aware of the exposure and take precautions. Watch for additional symptoms. If you answered "yes" to two or more, you may already be infected, and you need to receive a diagnosis from a professional to get your cure.

Ask yourself these additional questions:

- Are you able to make more than the minimum payments on your credit cards each month?
- Can you realistically predict a date within the next 36 months when your credit card or medical bills will be paid in full?
- Do you currently have money in a savings account?

If you answered "no" to any of these questions, in addition to any "yes" answers from above, you are experiencing financial crisis. Obtain the truth about your options. Seek the assistance of a bankruptcy professional in your community to review your specific circumstances.

THE ADVANTAGES OF WIPING OUT DEBT

- The money you were paying toward credit cards will now be yours.
- You'll be completely free of debt and the stress that comes with it.
- Your net worth will increase by the amount of debt you discharge.
- You can escape from bad real estate investments and unwise vehicle purchases.
- You may even be able to discharge taxes you owe the IRS.

CHAPTER THREE

IGNORING THE WARNING SIGNS

I believe that banking institutions are more dangerous
to our liberties than standing armies.
If the American people ever allow private banks
to control the issue of their currency,
first by inflation, then by deflation,
those banks and the corporations
that will grow up around the banks
will deprive the people of all property
until their children wake-up homeless
on the continent their fathers conquered.

— THOMAS JEFFERSON —

Serious illness devastates the body and mind and steals the patient's joy for life. When your body is sick, it's usually an indication that something is wrong. Ignoring these symptoms is foolish and potentially life-threatening. Overwhelming and insurmountable consumer debt is a serious financial illness.

Many pay no attention to their symptoms, hoping for a miracle cure that never comes. Others try self-medication: second jobs, home equity loans, liquidation of savings and retirement accounts, or frequent borrowing from relatives. Observers with no experience advise them how "wrong" bankruptcy is, and the financial charlatans who continue deriving profits from the disease chant "bankruptcy is your last resort."

Smart patients choose life over financial death, joy over financial misery, and financial freedom over financial bondage. They will recognize the different stages of this illness and take steps to begin the cure.

THE STAGES OF FINANCIAL ILLNESS

STAGE ONE: THE BUG THAT'S GOING AROUND

Stage One of financial illness is much like having a bad cough, a severe headache, or some other symptom of illness you believe will go away by itself if you just wait long enough.

The patient is current with all monthly debt obligations, but only makes the minimum payment each month and is making no progress towards financial health. The patient ignores the other symptoms completely—no savings, no foreseeable date when he will be debt-free, depleting retirement accounts to pay debt, transferring balances from one card to another to temporarily save on interest rates.

He is deluded into believing he needs no treatment and that the medication will make him worse. Absent treatment, the patient's condition may remain at Stage One, but will likely progress to Stage Two.

Bill and Teresa: Livin' The Dream

Bill and Teresa worked full time, had good-paying jobs, and drove nice cars. They lived in a beautiful home nestled in a gated community. They seem to have accumulated all the material things people could possibly want. Although their credit card debt was a significant amount ($85,000) and spread over numerous accounts, they were able to pay the minimum payments on each card every month without impacting their living expenses.

Bill had $12,000 in his 401(k) plan and Teresa had $2,000 in a Roth IRA she opened a few years ago. Neither had contributed anything to either account for several years because they were unable to divert any money from their car and credit card payments. Because their home had appreciated in value so much a few years ago, they embraced the astounding equity appreciation as their new retirement vehicle.

Last year Bill's employer reduced his hours at work, and Teresa was laid off indefinitely. After her unemployment benefits ran out, Teresa liquidated her IRA to make a mortgage payment. The next month, Bill took out a loan against his 401(k) to cover the mortgage, car, and credit card payments. He took out another 401(k) loan a few months later for the same reason. Now he cannot borrow any more and is struggling because his employer is deducting funds from his paycheck to repay these loans.

Teresa started working again, but her income is less than it was before. They recently learned that the equity in their home vanished faster than it accrued. Several times a month they each receive in the mail offers from credit card companies to transfer balances at a teaser interest rate. It made sense to save money with less interest, they reasoned, so they filled out the applications and sent them in. They struggled to keep track of each new account and missed payments on one, triggering a default interest rate of 29.99%. They still managed to cover their monthly obligations with difficulty, but they have no savings—and no idea when they will be out of debt.

Bill jokingly told his dad that he may have to file bankruptcy if things didn't change soon, but his dad always goes into a diatribe about how awful bankruptcy is and that, "We've always paid our bills no matter what." His brother Barney filed several years ago and has been ostracized ever since. Bill and Teresa are deeply into Stage One of financial illness. They should explore and seriously consider treatment as soon as possible.

STAGE TWO: LOSING CONSCIOUSNESS

Stage Two of financial illness is more serious, like frequent fainting spells or chronic, severe coughing. The patient is no longer able to maintain all of his or her monthly debt obligations but hopes for a miracle cure. Unable to make the minimum monthly credit card payments on time any longer, the patient watches helplessly as, one by one, each of her credit issuers increases her interest rate to levels a loan shark might envy. Contact from creditors is frequent and unpleasant and will only get worse. Her relatives loan her money periodically but make it clear they cannot do so indefinitely. She believes there is a way out, but cannot find it.

> *Before borrowing money from a friend,*
> *decide which you need most.*
>
> — AMERICAN PROVERB —

Penelope: Loyal and Responsible

Penelope did very well as a real estate agent. She believed her income would increase and be indefinite. She was able to buy the German sports sedan she had always coveted and could always make the substantial monthly payment. She paid little attention to the fact that her credit card debt kept growing with her lifestyle because she had little difficulty paying each month and sometimes paid her cards down substantially.

My credit card companies love me, she thought. *I am a responsible and loyal customer.* When the real estate market began its downward spiral, Penelope rode down with it. At first she only missed one card payment. Although she paid the late fee and sent the minimum payment as soon as she could, Goliath Bank raised her interest rate to the default level of 29.99%. Soon she missed another payment, this time with Monopoly Bank. They also raised her interest to the default rate of 29.99% after charging her a late fee and an over-limit fee.

Each time she called the card issuer and protested that she had been a good customer for years and had always paid her bills on time. Why were they doing this to such a loyal customer? She learned what few but all should know—you may be loyal to them, but they are not loyal to you.

Penelope then contacted a debt-consolidation company advertised on television. The actors portraying satisfied clients seemed happy and sincere, and the promise to help was compelling. She sent several hundred dollars and an application, thinking she had a repayment plan in effect. A few months later, she received a call from one of her credit card companies, who advised her that they had received no money from the debt consolidation agency. She pulled her credit report and discovered that all of her accounts were still being reported as delinquent, and she wondered how long it would be before she could reestablish any credit at all.

Everything she had ever heard about bankruptcy was bad, particularly that she wouldn't be able to get credit again for seven years. This sounded like a worse predicament than the one she was in so she decided not to explore her options. Her job situation worsened, and soon she was unable to make her car payments on time. Her parents loaned her money several times so her car would not be repossessed, but each time she had to call them for help she became a little more depressed.

Penelope is deeply into Stage Two of financial illness and needs treatment as soon as possible.

STAGE THREE: STOPPING THE BLEEDING

Stage Three of financial illness is like experiencing severe hemorrhaging. The patient is in serious financial jeopardy, overcome with panic, and does not know what to do. One or more creditors have already filed lawsuits. He hides his automobile at the neighbor's so it won't get repossessed while he sleeps. He refuses to answer his telephone because any call could be from a collection agency or attorney. Mail sits on the table unopened and ignored. His wages are being garnished. He's bounced several checks because his bank account was garnished. He should have sought treatment months ago and regrets that he ignored a friend's advice to meet with a bankruptcy attorney.

You can run, but you can't hide.

— JOE LOUIS —

Ricky

Ricky's divorce left him with thousands of dollars of credit card debt he and his former wife incurred while they were married. Although he managed to make ends meet working full-time, his income wasn't enough to cover all his living expenses and still pay much, if anything, toward the credit cards. Ricky tried to make payment arrangements at first but gave up and concluded that if he moved and changed his telephone number frequently, no one would be able to find him to collect the money.

The first judgment was obtained against him because the creditor knew where he worked and served him with a summons in the presence of his coworkers. One of them suggested Ricky talk to the same bankruptcy lawyer that had helped him get rid of his financial problems, but Ricky had always heard that filing bankruptcy was the worst thing you could do and paid no attention.

Ricky mistakenly believed the creditor couldn't do anything to him, so he didn't take the lawsuit seriously. Then his landlord informed him that the rent check bounced. Ricky's bank account had been garnished as a result of the judgment, and he now found himself delinquent on his rent and penniless until his next payday. He reluctantly approached his boss about a payroll advance and was stunned to learn the same creditor who'd cleaned out his bank account was now seeking to garnish his wages. His boss suggested that Ricky may want to start looking for another job.

The feeling of despair was familiar to Ricky. It was the same feeling he had when he and his former wife fought about money. He felt as helpless now as he did then. He didn't know life could get worse after his divorce, but it did. On more than one occasion Ricky contemplated death as the only solution to his predicament. He was deeply in Stage Three of financial illness and should have sought treatment months ago.

If it isn't the sheriff, it's the finance company;
I've got more attachments on me than a vacuum cleaner.

— JOHN BARRYMORE —

THERE *IS* HOPE

Fortunately none of these patients is terminal, and they can all be saved. In fact, most people with severe financial illness can be saved and cured completely if they don't continue to ignore their symptoms. If you are experiencing anything like Bill, Teresa, Penelope, or Ricky, stop ignoring your symptoms and seek treatment immediately.

Faith is taking the first step
even when you don't see the whole staircase.

— MARTIN LUTHER KING, JR. —

FINDING YOUR WARNING SIGNS

- Have you had any similar experiences like Bill and Teresa, Penelope, or Ricky?
- Highlight any facts you identify with in their stories.
- Highlight any parts of the three stages that apply to you.
- What stage do you think you are in?
- Is your spouse in a different stage than you?
- Share your insights with your spouse, then thank your spouse for their insight. This is important information for your relationship as well as for your financial future.

THE TRUTH

Denial ain't just a river in Egypt.

— Mark Twain —

INTRODUCTION

Money and debt have far more impact in our lives than just being dollars and cents on a bank statement. Our feelings of elation, desperation, shame, pride, fear and infallibility are strongly tied to how we perceive our financial situation. So, too, financial crisis comes at us from various directions. If we are not aware of it, our perception may be clouded and we may be deprived of the truth behind our financial condition.

And after all, it is the truth that we must have to get the cure.

First are the financial symptoms. These are facts—how much money and debt we have, our ability to pay all our bills on time, whether our car has been repossessed and how close we are to foreclosure.

Equally important is our emotional reaction—but not the obvious twist in our gut. No, it's those tricky little defense mechanisms we're unaware of clicking in to save the day. Unfortunately those defense mechanisms can deprive us of understanding the truth.

Remember how I described the chest pain and loss of vision when I was having a heart attack? What soon followed were the defense mechanisms—denial—*not me, I'm too young, I'm a vegetarian, I work out,* etc. Those are the things we tell ourselves that deny the truth about what is really going on.

What follows are the universal stages our clients experience in coming to grips with their financial circumstances.

CHAPTER FOUR

THE EMOTIONAL STAGES OF FINANCIAL CRISIS AND RECOVERY[1]

1. **The Comfort Zone.** In The Comfort Zone, people may be unaware of the consequences of being financially naive. Living within their means, they are not spending all of their disposable income. They save money, and think about starting a retirement plan. New credit cards are shoved into their wallets without regard to the interest rate. Minimum payments seem inconsequential; and sometimes balances can be paid off every month. Mortgages are manageable. Favorite pastimes include planning for major purchases, a new home or exotic vacations. As these dreams transform into reality, The Comfort Zone is left behind for the next stage.

2. **Denial/Defiance of warning signs and symptoms of financial crisis.** People will find themselves rationalizing away their symptoms. So long as they can open new accounts to shift balances and pay minimum monthly payments, they continue to accrue debt without regard to the consequence to their financial health. If you are aware of the warning signs, this is the time to see a bankruptcy professional.

3. **The Blame Game.** Whether they blame themselves, their employer, their kids, or their spouse, critical relationships begin to deteriorate. Marriages and family relationships suffer. Jobs are lost. Addictive behaviors surface such as alcohol and drug abuse. There may be outbursts of violence and rage. Seeing a bankruptcy professional at this point may be instrumental in halting further damage to families.

4. **Panic and Self-Help.** With creditors calling, late bills stacking up, law suits and repossessions being threatened, desperate consumers attempt to take control by liquidating their retirement accounts, home equity, and life insurance policies. They look for money to pay their creditors without regard to the long-term consequence to their financial future. They ask family members for loans, sometimes repeatedly. Credit counselors may be contacted who appear to offer hope but often provide little help. If a bankruptcy professional is contacted, valuable assets can be protected rather than being turned over to creditors. Yet for someone in

this stage, calling a bankruptcy attorney is not an option when they mistakenly *think* they know what they need to do and believe they don't need help. This decision is a tragic one for their financial future.

5. **Fear and Shame.** People feel like failures. Embarrassed, they try to keep their financial issues a secret. They are afraid to see a bankruptcy professional because they believe they should be able to figure it out for themselves. They may believe their religion forbids walking away from their debts. Ethically, they feel they should pay everything back. They are afraid that bankruptcy will prevent them from rebuilding their lives. Some believe they are losing an empire—a fantasy life which is nothing more than an illusion. They never owned most of it in the first place—the bank did. Most of our clients enter our office in this stage. They come in having exhausted every other option they can think of.

6. **Acceptance.** While this person or couple is able to see the severity of their financial situation, they are ready for a new chapter in their lives. They begin to get excited about breathing in the fresh air of living debt-free. Most of our clients leave our initial consultation in this stage with even more joy instilled by the time their case is concluded. We can only imagine how people's lives would be improved if they came into our office in this stage.

7. **The Awareness Zone.** Grateful for financial forgiveness, these consumers are hyper-vigilant to any financial pitfalls awaiting them. They carefully consider each

purchase. I*s this a need or a want? Does this purchase fit within my daily budget for expenses? Does this purchase help me meet my goals or move away from my goals?* People in The Awareness Zone are careful not to repeat the same patterns that caused them to drift out of The Comfort Zone into Denial. They:

- Know credit cards are not currency, but contracts to enter into a loan.

- Do not carry a credit card unless the purchase has been pre-planned at least 48 hours in advance.

- Carry only the amount of cash a daily budget permits

- At the end of each day, put what's left into a savings jar.

- Every night put the next day's cash allotment in the wallet.

Without utilizing a new strategy founded in financial awareness, people may drift back into any of the earlier emotional stages of financial crisis.

FINDING YOUR TRUTH

- What stage do you think your spouse is in?
- What stage best describes your actions?
- Can you foresee the ability to move through these stages by better understanding your options?

A journey of a thousand miles begins with one step.

— Confucius —

THE DEBTOR'S TRIANGLE

I once was lost but now am found,
was blind but now I see.

— John Newton —

Many people have been lost at sea in a place known as the Devil's Triangle. Some know it as the Bermuda Triangle where ships and airplanes have mysteriously disappeared without explanation. While many scientists discount any supernatural forces at work, it is reported that several forces converge in this area that are ingredients for disaster—magnetic anomalies combined with strong currents and unpredictable human behavior.

Similarly people who find themselves in a sea of debt often lose their way in The Debtor's Triangle. Their compass doesn't seem to work anymore. What they thought was North is really South. They are disoriented and don't trust the instruments they once relied upon. They feel ill and exhibit unusual physical symptoms. They make decisions that make little sense to those looking in from the outside. They find themselves in a very perilous situation in deep, dark water—alone.

The pyramid depicted on the dollar bill can serve as a reminder of the principles of The Debtor's Triangle. The dollar's pyramid was intended to have a much different meaning than the principle explained here, but from now on, we hope that when you see the pyramid it will remind you of how your financial stability impacts your viewpoint of the world.

Pyramids represent strength and endurance derived from the triangles that form their shape. Note the eye at the peak—able to see from the highest point because of the strong structure of the configuration. Imagine that each side of the triangle represents the three sides of every debtor—their cash flow, their physical self, and their reaction to their financial situation—**Financial CPR.**

- **C**ash Flow. When cash flow diminishes, people feel more desperate and less confident. One side of the triangle begins to crumble, weakening the whole structure. The peak, or the eye, will not have the same view it does as when cash flow is strong. The eye will see from a different vantage point rather than from the highest point.

- **P**hysical Self. If the side of the physical self begins to deteriorate from financial troubles with illness, ulcers, headaches, lack of sleep, then two sides of the triangle crumble, collapsing the structure and dropping the view of the eye even lower, preventing the highest and best viewpoint.

- **Reaction.** Reaction encompasses people's emotions that flow from their financial situation and the resulting impact on their relationships. If you have ever seen a stock climb in your portfolio, you may be familiar with the feeling of elation that comes from believing you are financially set. If you've ever seen your portfolio plummet, you know the sick feeling in the pit of your stomach just from looking at the numbers on your statement. If the reaction side of the triangle begins to crumble, so crumbles the entire structure, and there is no elevated viewpoint. Personal goals and aspirations may be impacted because one's overall viewpoint of the world is impaired.

If your cash flow is decreasing, you are exhibiting physical symptoms, *and* your reaction to your financial situation is impacting your relationships—all three sides of The Debtor's Triangle collapse into a pile of rubble.

The Debtor's Triangle illustrates the principle that cash flow, or lack of cash, becomes more serious when it is coupled with physical symptoms and emotional symptoms. When two or more factors combine, they deteriorate and destroy the foundation that provides the highest and best view of our lives. But it can be rebuilt.

Financial CPR restores your cash flow, lessens physical symptoms attributed to the stress of your financial situation and restores the relationships suffering from your economic situation.

"My wife Mary and I have been married
for forty-seven years and not once have we had
an argument serious enough to consider divorce;
murder, yes, but divorce, never."

— JACK BENNY —

Will and Gina: A Price Too High

Will and Gina seemed like the typical married couple. They'd been married for almost twenty years, had three terrific children, and appeared to be very successful. Gina worked for a large insurance company and made a good salary. Will, however, owned his own business—a coffee shop franchise. They had two mortgages on their home and no equity. They were also in serious financial peril.

The coffee shop had been a dream of Will's for a long time. After working for the same company for many years, Will had accumulated a sizeable 401(k) account. The house he and Gina owned had appreciated in value substantially in the early stages of the real estate bubble. Their financial future seemed pretty secure, and the pieces of their "dream" puzzle seemed to be coming together. One day they took the leap of faith so many do, and Will quit his job to open the shop.

It was easy to get a loan from the Small Business Administration to buy equipment. Getting a second mortgage to purchase the franchise rights was easier. Within a few months, Will was able to open his own business at last.

The shop did well at first. Will was able to cover all his expenses and pay himself a small salary. But when the economy started its rapid slide, the shop began to experience less and less traffic, and Will's business was no longer profitable. At first he thought it was a temporary downturn, but each month his profit dwindled below the previous month's.

Because he had to pay his franchisor, his landlord, and the SBA every month no matter what, he and Gina started to draw on the home equity line of credit to make ends meet. When they reached the loan limit, Will began withdrawing money from his 401(k) account. Month after month, Will observed other franchises just like his close, but he was convinced his shop would be different. He had a core of regular customers, and he felt an obligation to them. He also didn't want to give up on his dream. He was in serious denial.

It was important for me to spend a little more time explaining the options Will and Gina had to obtain the financial help they so desperately needed. I patiently went over every detail and scenario my experience could provide them with. I finished my analysis and discussion of their unique situation and told them what I recommended. They seemed relieved and happy at the prospect of freeing themselves from their horrible financial predicament.

This is typically the best part of my meetings with clients. The darkness lifts, the rain stops, and contemplating a future without crushing debt drains the pent-up stress these poor folks have suffered for too long.

Then Will dropped a bombshell. "There's one more thing you need to know," he said, after I was sure we had covered everything thoroughly. I always hate it when clients start their sentences like that; usually it means I'm about to hear something really bad. I was right.

Tears began to well up in his eyes as he softly told me that Gina had filed for divorce. The overwhelming debt that had accumulated as the result of Will's business failing had taken a tremendous emotional toll on Gina. She had decided that her life would be better without Will and all the financial problems he had inadvertently created with his business.

The one statistic that haunts my memory came flooding back: approximately eighty percent of the divorces in our country are caused by financial problems. Twenty years and thousands of clients have demonstrated this to me time and time again. Couples who genuinely love each other and have created beautiful families together are torn apart by dollars and cents, replaceable things, and the vision of a grand lifestyle that is pushed on us from early adulthood.

Although we are Counselors at Law we also become "Counselors at Life" from time to time. We receive no training for this in law school, and some of us are better at it than others. Compassion is the foundation; experience is the vehicle.

I told Will and Gina the disheartening statistic about debt and divorce. Then I asked them to do something I probably had no business requesting. "Let's file this case as soon as we can. When the phone calls stop, the creditors stop harassing you, and you aren't bleeding cash anymore, see how this impacts your day-to-day interaction with each other." I hoped my words were not in vain. "The worst thing that can possibly happen is that if you do decide to go forward with the divorce, all these debts will be gone, and you will have one less issue to fight about when the time comes."

I could tell both of them had listened with great interest. I went on. "The best thing that could happen is you realize that your marriage can be saved if you get rid of all these external destructive forces battering it every day." Sometimes this advice works and sometimes it doesn't, but it sure is worth trying.

One Saturday afternoon early in my legal career, I was working in my yard when the mail truck pulled up. I heard a voice yell my name. It was a substitute mail carrier filling in for ours who was on vacation. I went to see who he was and how he knew me. As I got closer, I recognized him but couldn't recall his name.

"Do you remember me? My wife and I were clients of yours a few years ago. You did our Chapter 7 case for us. I want you to know that listening to you and filing that case was the best thing that ever happened to us. It saved our marriage. Thank you so much."

I was astounded. As he pulled away and I resumed my solitary gardening duties, I realized what a tremendously positive impact becoming debt-free can have on people and their relationships. That one client sharing his joy with me was one of the greatest rewards I have had in my professional career, and I will always remember that day as if it were yesterday.

The Debtor's Triangle is very real. It can be fragile, as with Will and Gina who had cash flow problems, physical symptoms of exhaustion and depression, and reactions of anger and resentment. Or it can be strong, as with my mail carrier client who restored his cash flow, became stress-free, and reacted with a newfound commitment to his wife and family.

FINDING YOUR TRUTH

- The three sides of The Debtor's Triangle are cash flow, physical symptoms, and your reactions. Is any one side of your triangle beginning to deteriorate?
- How is your cash flow?
- Are you having physical symptoms? Could they be caused by the stress of your financial problems?
- Are your relationships suffering because of your financial issues?
- Is your view of the world impacted because of your cash flow, physical symptoms, and your reaction to your finances?
- Can you envision any aspect of the three sides of The Debtor's Triangle improving if your debts were forgiven?
- Can you envision your view of the world improving if any side of The Debtor's Triangle was restored in your life?

CHAPTER SIX

SNAKE-OIL SALESMEN

The devil made me do it.

— FLIP WILSON —

Before the advent of modern medicine, many who were seriously ill relied upon concoctions purchased from strangers who traveled from town to town in a wagon. The "snake oil" they sold was good for the salesmen but did nothing to cure the buyer and often made him worse. Many narcotics regulated by federal law today were once available on the open market for anyone to purchase. The widespread availability of these drugs made the consumer temporarily feel good but threatened to create a nation of addicts.

Today's financially ill face similar challenges when seeking a cure. It is hard to know who to trust, particularly when those offering the "helping hand" may really be representing your creditors, not you.

Max and the Debt Consolidator

Max has been married for three years. It was important to him that he and his wife quickly acquire the paraphernalia of success and happiness. Credit cards came quickly and easily, and they took advantage of them all. Like many, Max worried only about making the minimum payments on each account. Some day he would have a bigger income and would be able to pay everyone in full. But the pay raises were few and far between, and soon he found it increasingly difficult to make the payments. Max and his wife began arguing more frequently, and Max had trouble sleeping.

While surfing the Internet one day, Max saw an advertisement for a debt consolidation program. It promised to negotiate lower interest rates, reduce his monthly payments, and combine all his credit card debts into one "easy" payment. He quickly signed up and began having $500 a month automatically drafted from his checking account.

Nine months later, he spoke to a mortgage broker about refinancing his house to pay everything off. The broker pulled his credit report and called Max with bad news. The debt consolidation company had made several payments on Max's credit cards—late. His credit scores were no better than when he started the debt consolidation plan. Also, even though he was paying $500 a month, only $425 was being applied to his credit cards. The debt consolidation company didn't tell Max they received a 15% fee each month from his payment. They also didn't tell him that they might pay his accounts late from time to time.

> *Fool me once, shame on you.*
> *Fool me twice, shame on me.*
> — Chinese Proverb —

Sheila and the Pleasant Creditor's Attorney

Sheila was nervous the morning she had to appear in court for a pre-trial conference. She had no experience with these things and didn't know what to expect. The attorney for her creditor obtained a final judgment against her, but he seemed friendly and sympathetic and even offered to set up a payment plan. All he asked for was $25 per week to pay a reduced amount of the judgment.

Sheila signed a paper the attorney brought with him and wrote a check for $25. For the first three months she was able to send the attorney the agreed-upon payment, but being a single parent with two small children and sporadic support payments from her former husband made it difficult when unexpected expenses came up. The first time she missed a payment, Sheila received a call from the lawyer's office. She was able to borrow enough from her mother to make the payment but was no longer able to send money after that. The telephone calls stopped, but she kept getting letters from the lawyer's office—which she didn't open, because she didn't know what to do.

Sheila finally had some good news. Her income tax refund would be $2,300. She desperately needed the money for so many things. When the money finally arrived, she deposited it into her account and immediately began writing checks.

Soon she began receiving notices from the bank charging her a bounced-check fee. Sheila couldn't understand why the checks she wrote for her mortgage, car and home insurance were returned for non-sufficient funds. What she didn't know was that by providing the stream of checks at $25 per week, she had given the attorney the name, location and account number of her bank account.

Patiently he waited until Sheila was no longer making payments. Then once she deposited her tax refund, the creditor seized his opportunity. The next day, a writ of garnishment was presented to the manager of Sheila's bank, and the $2,300 tax refund was gone in an instant.

The Handy-Dandy Payday Loan

Now Sheila's financial difficulties became financial nightmares. She began getting loans from one of those companies that offer "payday advances" to those in dire financial straits. She quickly discovered that attempting to repay the loans at their horrific interest rates depleted her paychecks more and more each pay period. When she finally realized that she was borrowing against her paycheck six weeks in the future just to repay the loan she'd obtained six weeks in the past, she became despondent.

Max and Sheila are both suffering very common financial afflictions and both see no end to their seemingly endless cycles of misery. Both can be released from their financial despair and begin to enjoy their lives again if they make the right choice.

Time extensions, lower interest rates, waiving late fees, and outright forgiveness of large amounts of debt are becoming more common now because consumers simply cannot pay anymore. Realizing that we are on the verge of an economic tsunami, creditors are trying to collect as much as they can while there are still a few dollars left to collect. While the concessions they offer may seem like a life preserver to someone drowning financially, the reality may be that your creditor is finding more ways to get more money out of you before you run totally dry.

When you seek the advice of a specialist in bankruptcy, you are grabbing a life preserver with someone at the other end of the rope who can save you. They can pull you out of the ocean, dry you off and take you to shelter. Most importantly, bankruptcy gives you a second chance at the life you dreamed of.

Gotcha: Martha's Mountain Getaway

Martha has a vacation rental she owns in the mountains. Several weeks passed since she last visited her place, and she was excited to go again. As she walked through the front door, she noticed her answering machine blinking. When she played the messages, she found seventeen all saying the same thing, like a recording.

"This is a call for Jackson Smith. If you are Jackson Smith, press one. Pressing one acknowledges that you are, in fact, Jackson Smith. You may return this call by dialing 1-888-888-8888. When you reach an account representative, give them your account number, which is the same as your social security number, so they may pull your file. Thank you."

What is this? she thought. *I've never heard of Jackson Smith. I've never rented the place to a Jackson Smith. I don't want these people calling here anymore. I sure don't want to talk to them, and I don't want them hassling my tenants.*

Just then the phone rang. It was the same recording. "If you are Jackson Smith, press one. Pressing one acknowledges that you are, in fact, Jackson Smith." Martha wanted to press one and tell these people not to call any more, but she knew she might have trouble explaining that she really wasn't Jackson Smith if she admitted to it by pressing one.

What a pain in the neck! She hung up. Martha had no way of knowing whether this was, indeed, an attempt to collect a debt, although it certainly sounded like it.

Martha went to the Internet and looked up the phone number on her caller ID. It was tied to another phone number allegedly for a collection agency. She called them, explained that she was getting the calls for Jackson Smith, whom she didn't know, and told them to stop calling her number. She informed them that any further calls would be in violation of the Federal Fair Debt Collection Practices Act, and she would take action against them.

Martha was smart to do so. This was a clever tactic taken by this collection agency.

Had Jackson Smith answered the phone rather than Martha, and had he pressed one and provided his social security number, he would have provided one of the most valuable pieces of information a creditor needs to execute a judgment against him. It's unlikely that his account number had anything to do with his social security number.

As a matter of fact, Jackson Smith could have returned a call to a company posing as a collection agency that was, instead, trying to steal his identity. If he knew he owed nothing, he may have provided the information in an attempt to clear his name. In fact, he could have given his identity away to thieves.

When people call, there is no way to know where they are calling from, much less whether they are who they say they are. It is best to assume they are *not* who they say they are. You are not required to give anyone any information about yourself over the phone. Turn the tables. Demand *their* name, their contact information, their address, the name of their employer, and their supervisor. Verify independently who they are. Never give out any information to someone you don't know.

Creditors are permitted to act within the law to legally collect what is owed them, however it is important to understand what creditors are not permitted to do to collect on a debt. If you are wondering about your consumer rights, check out www.ftc.gov where the Federal Trade Commission provides information on a variety of subjects, including The Fair Debt Collection Practices Act to protect you, the consumer.

THE FAIR DEBT COLLECTION PRACTICES ACT

The Fair Debt Collection Practices Act[2] precludes the following types of collection activity:

- Third parties cannot be contacted (with the exception of a debtor's attorney or credit bureau) other than to locate the debtor. The third parties must state their names and indicate they are confirming or correcting information about the debtor.

- Collection agents cannot provide their agency names unless asked.

- Collection agents cannot repeatedly contact a third party unless there is reason to believe information provided earlier was wrong or incomplete.

- Collection agents cannot use correspondence with words or symbols that misrepresent their intent to collect a debt.

- If a debtor is represented by counsel, a collection agency cannot contact the debtor unless the debtor gives them specific permission to do so.

- If the collection agent is advised that an employer bans receipt of collection calls at work, a debtor cannot be contacted on the job.

- Collection agents may not call before 8 AM or after 9 PM.

- Collection agents may not threaten violence or use profane language.

- Collection agents cannot publish a debtor's name on a public black list or posting.

- Collection agents cannot threaten criminal prosecution or threaten to seize property to which they have no right.

- Collection agents cannot lie about the debt or who they are.

- Collection agents cannot send documents that appear to be legal papers when they are not.

Do collection agents do these things? Some do. However they are very familiar with their responsibilities and will stop all collection activity when a bankruptcy case is filed. They can receive substantial fines in Bankruptcy Court for failing to cease all collection activity. If there is a history of abuse, they can get hit hard.

If you are receiving harassing calls, keep a diary of the date, time, name of the person, number from which they called, and what they said. Advise them not to call anymore, and if you are not in bankruptcy, follow up with those instructions in writing. If you are in bankruptcy, provide the information to your bankruptcy lawyer.

FINDING YOUR TRUTH

- Did you know that as part of the bankruptcy process, Bankruptcy Court requires you to have credit counseling with a court-approved credit counseling service?

- Have you considered seeing a credit counselor?

- Would you consider seeing a credit counselor as well as a bankruptcy attorney, since both are required before filing a bankruptcy, and the cost is minimal?

- Have you been asked to sign any agreements with your creditors because of being in default?

- Were you aware that the information you provide your creditors and their lawyers may be used to collect their debts?

- Have you ever considered getting a payday loan?

- Are you aware that the interest on a payday loan annualized can be from several hundred to over one thousand percent?

CHAPTER SEVEN

FORGIVE US OUR DEBTS

Forgive us our debts as we forgive our debtors.

— MATTHEW 6:12, KING JAMES BIBLE —

Guilt is one of the most powerful emotions we experience. Our conscience is reminding us of our inherent desire to "do the right thing." This is what makes us human. Many of the people who meet with us express this concern. They sincerely wish they could repay all of their debts, and the sooner the better. They recognize that they did, in fact, borrow all this money they owe. Many are consumed with guilt, remorse, and an inability to forgive themselves.

Some of our clients have based their reluctance to seek the financial relief they need on teachings within their chosen religion. Many religions implore their believers to repay any and all debts but also speak of forgiving the debts of others. One of the common precepts of most religions is the recognition that we are human, that humans are imperfect, humans make mistakes, and that humans should learn from their mistakes and strive to not repeat them.

Our clients who have agonized over their financial crisis recognized that they truly intended to repay their debts and made every effort to do so. But ultimately, no matter how hard they tried, no matter what they did, they simply could not do it. *Wanting* to do what is right, *but not being able to*, is totally different from being able to do what is right but refusing. Accepting that distinction is extremely important for this is what leads to a very important aspect of life—forgiving yourself.

If you aren't able to pay your debts and can file a bankruptcy in truth and honesty, you should be legally forgiven of your debt. That is what the law provides with roots deep in our faiths and cultures. Remember, if you feel a moral obligation to repay your debts after your discharge, you may do so in your own time and without contact from your creditors or any legal obligation to do so.

If we can forgive the CEO of a major bank who allegedly recently spent a fortune to redecorate his office, despite his bank losing tens of billions of dollars and getting taxpayer bailout money, we can certainly forgive the honest citizen who struggles day in and day out to survive.

> *To err is human, to forgive, divine.*
> — Alexander Pope (1688-1744 English Poet) —

FINDING YOUR TRUTH AND FORGIVING YOURSELF

As you go through the questions below, be honest with yourself and with your answers.

- Do you believe you have tried as hard as you can to repay your debts?

- Do you feel guilty or ashamed because you can't repay your debts?

- Do your religious beliefs make you hesitant to consider bankruptcy?

If you answered yes to any of these questions, remember this: our cultures and religions embrace forgiveness as a fundamentally important aspect of our humanity. Being unable to do something does not make you dishonest, unworthy or undeserving.

- When you were accumulating your debt over time, did you ever think to yourself, *I have no intention of paying any of this back?*

- Are you afraid of your loved ones' reactions?

- Do you believe your loved ones' feelings will change about you because of it?

- Do you foresee your partner's ability to forgive you for acquiring the debt? For failing to fully disclose it to them?

- Do you have spiritual beliefs that you believe keep you from seeking discharge of your debts?

- Do you understand that obtaining a legal discharge of your debts through bankruptcy still permits you to repay them if you feel you should?

The God I believe in is a God of second chances.

— BILL CLINTON —

CHAPTER EIGHT

AFFLUENZA[3]— THE MODERN-DAY DEBTOR'S PRISON

Debt is the slavery of the free.

— PUBLILIUS SYRUS —

Those who don't know about or ignore the warning signs of a serious illness do nothing to cure their disease. They may be slowly killing themselves without realizing it. When they find out they're very sick, many people continue risky behaviors anyway and refuse to take the remedy that will cure them.

We are brainwashed into believing that collecting lots of material things is and should be our life's main purpose. We admire and envy people who accumulate the most, and we see those that don't as failures. After we give in to the constant message of "more stuff means you are more successful," we surrender to the concept of perpetual debt, made easier by low monthly payments, which pay slightly more than the previous month's interest.

> *"Every day I get up and look through the Forbes list of the richest people in America. If I'm not there, I go to work."*
>
> — ROBERT ORBEN —

Tom and Desiree: Movin' on up

Tom and Desiree had been together since they met in college. After graduation, they got married and started their careers, eager to build their American dream. They bought a small town home they could afford, but the payments made their budget a little tight. Their old furniture just didn't make their new home look "new," so they went to a furniture store and bought new furniture for the whole house. The 18% interest rate wouldn't be a problem because they would make large payments to pay off the account quickly. They also decided to finance a new washer and dryer.

A few months later they realized that after paying the mortgage and covering their living expenses, they could only make the minimum payments on the furniture and appliance accounts. They still managed to make the payments on time even though they barely made a dent in the balances. A savings account for emergencies was just not possible.

They had lots of friends and noticed that most of them were doing much better than they were. Most had new big-screen TVs, expensive stereos, video game systems and the newest, most expensive cell phones. They all had lots of nice clothes, and most were driving nice, new cars. They kept getting the same message over and over on TV, in magazines, on billboards and the internet: "Successful people have more stuff. You are not successful if you don't have lots of stuff."

It must be true, they thought. *Look at all of our friends and neighbors.* Desiree's boss always reminded her that "the one who dies with the most toys wins."

Right after Desiree was promoted, she was convinced it was very important to improve her image. She bought a new car to replace the old one her parents gave her in college. Then she decided she needed new clothes for work which she charged on her new department store accounts. Tom's job was going well too. His commissions were increasing, and once in awhile he received a nice, fat bonus. Tom also thought he needed to improve his image, so he bought a new sports car and new clothes. For Christmas they bought a plasma-screen TV for their living room, and they got each other expensive watches.

As their income grew, so did their spending. The credit card companies must have thought they were great customers, because they kept increasing the limits. Every once in awhile they would get a little nervous when they opened their statements because the balances kept getting bigger and bigger.

No problem, they thought. *We can make the minimum payments on all of our credit cards because we're making more money than we used to. In the future we will make even more money, and someday we'll pay those cards off.*

Tom and Desiree noticed that many of their friends were buying new, bigger houses. They were actually embarrassed to have company over because they thought their old town home was cramped and dated. So they bought a beautiful house in a new subdivision, much bigger and more impressive than their town home. Because of their debt situation, Tom and Desiree had to go with an adjustable rate mortgage and relied on having a dependable renter in their old townhouse to cover that payment.

The mortgage broker told them not to worry about the payment going up in two years. He promised them he would refinance it then and get them a better deal. The house would be worth so much more in two years that refinancing would be easy. The day they closed on their new home seemed like the best day of their lives together, and they celebrated at their favorite restaurant with a bottle of champagne.

Tom and Desiree had their dream house, a rental property, new cars, lots of nice clothes, and lots of electronic gadgets. They were proud of themselves for reaching the "top of the mountain." Tom's brother, Cecil, wasn't as lucky. Cecil worked hard, but his job didn't pay very well. Whenever Cecil and his wife visited, the two were uncomfortable because they didn't have the nice things or the big house that Tom and Desiree had. Tom showed Cecil all the new stuff he had gotten since the last visit. The drive home was always depressing for Cecil and his wife because they couldn't afford to buy the "stuff" everyone else had. Soon the visits from Cecil stopped.

> *Debt is like any other trap, easy enough to get into,*
> *but hard enough to get out of.*
>
> — HENRY WHEELER SHAW —

It wasn't until Tom was laid off for awhile that he and Desiree discovered the truth about their lifestyle. The mountain they were on top of was a mountain of debt. Covering their living expenses from Desiree's paychecks wasn't easy. The money was gone as fast as it went into their account. They argued when there wasn't any money for unexpected expenses. They couldn't take an inexpensive vacation unless they put it on a credit card.

Week after week, month after month, they struggled to keep all their payments current. They thought they owned many beautiful, expensive things. In reality, their beautiful expensive things owned them. Their debt had become the walls of their financial prison.

Since every dollar they earned was gone right away, they had no money put away for an emergency, like Tom getting laid off from his job. Not having his income created a financial emergency. They had to choose between paying the mortgage and paying their other debts. They argued a lot.

Their parents bailed them out a few times, but it was humiliating to ask for help. Tom managed to find another job, but it paid a lot less, and they were behind on all of their credit card payments. Then the renter moved out of their old house, and they couldn't find anyone to move in.

Tom and Desiree were in serious financial trouble. Their climb to the top of the mountain of success had been slow and difficult. Falling down was fast and painful. Their arguments were more frequent and ugly. These two loved each other so much they planned to spend the rest of their lives together. Now they barely spoke except for arguing.

Their dream house went into foreclosure first, and their old house wasn't far behind. The calls from the credit card companies were frequent and unpleasant. When Desiree's boss lectured her about getting too many calls at work, she broke down and cried. The mortgage payments, the car payments and the credit cards had become shackles and chains. Their American Dream had become a nightmare.

Juan and Jacinta: Thrifty and Conservative

Juan and Jacinta were a lot different than Tom and Desiree. They were thrifty shoppers. They always went to Target or Wal-Mart when they needed something. They drove older cars and lived in a small house. They only had one credit card, but when they bought something, they always charged it. Their purchases were usually limited to burgers at McDonalds, prescriptions, and sometimes groceries.

The balance on the account was usually around $5,000, and the interest rate was 18%. Each month they tried to pay at least $100 on the account, but they could never get the balance below $5,000. One day they decided they would stop using the credit card and start paying cash for everything. Jacinta thought that by paying $100 each month, they would have the account paid off in a little over four years.

In fact, it would take ninety-four months to pay the balance, and they would pay an additional $4,311 in interest on top of the $5,000 balance. The fast food, groceries and movie tickets were being paid for years after they were bought and ended up costing a lot more.[4]

> *Interest works night and day in fair weather and foul.*
> *It gnaws at man's substance with invisible teeth.*
>
> — SIMONE WEIL (1910–1943, FRENCH PHILOSOPHER) —

These couples fell into the same trap as many other people. Every day they were bombarded with the same messages:

- Your value as a person is measured by the value of your stuff. The less stuff you have, the less important you are.
- It's okay to buy stuff you can't afford because you can borrow the money. If it takes your whole life to pay it back, don't worry—that's okay too.

- It is responsible and frugal to make infrequent and strictly discount purchases with your credit cards while making only minimum payments every month.

Frugal purchases morph into huge debts, doubling or tripling the cost of the original purchase, depending on your interest rate, additional fees, and whether you carry a minimum balance. The truth—a purchase is not frugal if a balance is carried on a credit card.

I'm living so far beyond my income
that we may almost be said to be living apart.

— E.E. CUMMINGS (1894–1962) —

FINDING YOUR TRUTH

Do you see yourself in any of these situations?

- Are you trying to keep up?
- Are you constantly moving up the ladder of acquiring better things?
- Are you thrifty but charge budget purchases?
- Does it surprise you to know that paying a minimum balance can double or even triple the purchase price of your items, depending on your interest rate?

If the answer is "yes" to any of these questions, you are in today's version of Debtor's Prison. You are trapped by things you financed. The minimum monthly payments are the bars on the window. Your handcuffs are the interest you pay on stuff you bought long ago.

THE CURE

CHAPTER NINE

READ THE LABEL AND TAKE AS PRESCRIBED

Some debts are fun when you are acquiring them,
but none are fun when you set about retiring them.

— Ogden Nash —

Serious illness always requires treatment. Medications often have unwanted side effects, and surgery is always scary. Most people recognize that refusing treatment to avoid discomfort usually makes their situation much worse.

In much the same way that people fear shots or surgical procedures, people fear bankruptcy. This fear is often based on misconceptions, half-truths, and some down-right lies.

One common misconception about bankruptcy is that "you lose everything." The truth is that bankruptcy does not take everything away from you. Debtors are allowed to retain certain assets so they have what they need to begin their financial healing process, the most important of which are retirement savings governed by state and federal laws.

MYTHS, HALF-TRUTHS AND DOWN-RIGHT LIES ABOUT BANKRUPTCY

- They changed the law—you can't file any more.
- You aren't allowed to keep your house or any personal possessions.
- You can't have any money in the bank.
- You have to wait until you have used up everything you have saved.
- You can't discharge money you owe the IRS.
- It will ruin your credit score.
- You can't buy a house, car or get credit cards afterwards.
- You can't get approved for loans.
- You can't get a job.
- You can't rent.

DISPELLING THE MYTHS

Once you realize you have a serious financial problem, it is important to take the first step in the right direction. An experienced attorney specializing in bankruptcy law can help you do this. One of the most important services they will provide you is giving accurate information about assets you may keep and debts you can eliminate when you file. Many people get their "information" about bankruptcy from friends, neighbors, or coworkers who have never actually filed themselves but have "heard" all about it. They are eager to share all the knowledge they have accumulated, but much of it is incorrect.

BANKRUPTCY PROTECTION FOR INDIVIDUALS

For most individuals, there are two different types of relief available in bankruptcy—Chapter 7 and Chapter 13. "Chapter" refers to where the provisions are found within Title 11 of the United States Code, commonly known as the Bankruptcy Code. This book isn't meant to do more than give you a very basic idea of how each chapter works and the differences between the two. Your bankruptcy specialist will give you more detailed information relevant to your situation when you meet with him or her.

One of the most gratifying things about filing bankruptcy is the umbrella of protection you have from your creditors. It is called the "automatic stay." With very few exceptions, creditors are prohibited from calling you, writing to you, or harassing you in any way after you file. A bankruptcy specialist can explain how the automatic stay applies to you, which will allow you to sleep better at night.

CHAPTER 7 BANKRUPTCY:
QUICK AND EFFECTIVE

Chapter 7 works like a surgeon removing a tumor. It is done quickly, doesn't take very long, and you begin your recovery in a short period of time. The process usually takes four to six months after the case is filed, depending on where you live and where your case is filed. In most jurisdictions, you have to make an appearance at an administrative hearing called a "Meeting of Creditors." Your attorney goes with you.

The idea behind Chapter 7 is to eliminate or "discharge" as much debt as possible. The primary purpose is to eliminate consumer and medical debt you are unable to pay, but there are other categories of debt that may qualify. Even taxes owed the Internal Revenue Service may be discharged under certain circumstances. There are several types of debt you cannot discharge in Chapter 7, but these will be discussed between you and your bankruptcy specialist.

CHAPTER 13: FINANCIAL REHAB

Chapter 13 works like physical rehabilitation or therapy. It takes a period of time for the healing process to be completed, depending on the severity and type of financial illness being cured, but the process begins upon filing. Chapter 13 requires you to pay some or all of your creditors under the supervision and protection of the Bankruptcy Court. The monthly amount each creditor gets is based on what type of debt you owe them and how much you are able to pay after your living expenses are provided for.

Like rehabilitation or physical therapy, it requires your participation and determination to do what is necessary to be cured. Your bankruptcy attorney will assist along the way.

There comes a time in the affairs of man where he must take the bull by the tail and face the situation.

— W.C. FIELDS —

BANKRUPTCY IS *GOOD*

Bankruptcy is not meant to punish those who file; it's meant to help. Since the goal is to eliminate debt (with some exceptions your bankruptcy specialist will discuss with you), this should be the primary focus for anyone suffering serious financial illness. I know of no other sure-fire way to increase your net worth overnight other than filing bankruptcy.

THE MAIN STREET, USA BAILOUT

Bankruptcy is clearly a good option for those who have suffered a devastating illness or accident and are faced with staggering medical expenses they can't possibly pay. But why did Congress make it possible for Americans to eliminate their consumer debt by filing bankruptcy?

The intent of Congress was to provide the honest but unfortunate debtor an economic fresh start without the oppression of debt.[5] A discharge in bankruptcy allows the individual to once again become a "useful" member of society.

You hear repeatedly that America has a consumer-driven economy. This means our economic health depends on all of us going out and buying things on a regular basis.

Most people in financial distress are in a situation where they cannot spend anymore. They are so deeply in debt they can't buy a new car, refrigerator, or clothes. They can't take vacations, go out to dinner, or buy flowers for their sweetheart on Valentine's Day. Many take only half their medication because they can't afford to refill their prescriptions when the medication runs out.

When we reach a point where many of us are unable to buy anything because we've exhausted all our credit resources, we don't participate in the economy, and the economy suffers. When we jeopardize our retirement because we cannot save due to our perpetual debt, we become a burden on our families and the economy. Allowing honest people to discharge the debts that prevent them from participating in and nurturing our economy makes sense for the consumers, the manufacturers, the shippers, and the retailers.

YOU WON'T LOSE EVERYTHING

Little piglets are cute and lovely;
when they grow into hogs they get slaughtered.

— THE HONORABLE ALEXANDER L. PASKAY,
CHIEF BANKRUPTCY JUDGE EMERITUS
MIDDLE DISTRICT OF FLORIDA, TAMPA DIVISION —

"Losing everything" is a phrase we hear often when new clients are telling us some of the reasons they are afraid of bankruptcy. In fact, Congress specifically created a list of assets that can be kept when someone files for bankruptcy protection called "exemptions." Congress recognized the importance of allowing individuals to retain certain assets to begin their fresh start, so they crafted a list of certain things they felt were important for people to retain while seeking the relief they needed.

Each state's legislature was allowed to adopt the list of exempt assets drawn up by Congress or to draft a separate list of exempt assets deemed more suitable for residents of that particular state. Most have elected to create their own list of exemptions, and your bankruptcy specialist will discuss those available to you based on where you reside.

One important aspect to the exemption policy concerns retirement benefits. Legislators felt it was so important for people to retain funds designated for retirement that almost all types of retirement plans are exempt in bankruptcy. Again, your bankruptcy specialist will guide you with this issue.

Will They Take My Stuff?

Occasionally clients we see have more assets than they are allowed to exempt. Usually this doesn't create a major problem, and they are able to keep the excess "stuff" by paying the amount they go over their limit by. Sometimes, however, the amount of excess is too large, and the decision to let go of material possessions must be made.

Disclose, Disclose, Disclose

Whatever your concerns, make sure you disclose everything you own as well as everything you owe to your bankruptcy attorney. To properly assist you, your lawyer must be aware of all of your assets. You won't get the right advice if you're not completely honest. The solution to your problems lies in the truth. The truth shall, indeed, set you free—not to mention the fact that dishonesty can send you to jail.

Look to the future, because that is where you'll spend the rest of your life.

— GEORGE BURNS —

Kevin's Story: Letting Go

Kevin had been a successful mortgage broker since 2003. When he came to see me in early 2007, he was deeply in debt and hadn't closed many loans for several months. His credit cards were all maxed out, and he was getting so many calls he was afraid to answer his phone. But he had to answer each call because he couldn't afford to miss any potential new business. He lived in a modest house he bought in 2005, and he drove a late-model luxury car he had paid cash for in better times.

Kevin decided he needed to file for protection under Chapter 7 to eliminate all the credit card debt he had and to discharge the debt on the home he could no longer afford. All of this was a good thing, he realized. Under Florida's exemption statutes, Kevin was able to exempt everything he wanted to keep except his car.

When I explained that he would have to let it go in exchange for eliminating all his debts in Chapter 7, he told me without any hesitation that he didn't care about the car. He knew he could always get another one, and he recognized how much he needed to get the financial relief he would receive in exchange. It was an easy decision for him to make, and I commended him for being able to see it was a wise decision on his part.

Another way to solve the traffic problems of this country is to pass a law that only paid-for cars be allowed to use the highways.

— Will Rogers —

Alicia: Hangin' On

Alicia's financial problems were a lot like Kevin's. Her employer had cut her hours quite a bit, and she was barely able to meet all of her living expenses, let alone her credit card payments. Alicia had come to the United States from another country, and the car she was driving was the first she had ever owned. It took her awhile to finish paying it off and not having a monthly payment was a blessing.

But Alicia was maxed out on her credit cards, and she had a substantial number of medical bills she could not pay. Like Kevin, she would be able to exempt everything she had except her car. Unlike Kevin, however, Alicia could not bear the thought of having to let it go.

I explained to her that getting another car would not be difficult for her once her case was over. But Alicia was so emotionally attached to this particular automobile she first decided not to seek the relief she desperately needed. It took a few more months of constant harassment by creditors to finally convince Alicia that her desire to hang onto a "thing" that could be replaced was causing her considerable stress and anguish, and it was simply not worth it anymore. When the harassing calls stopped and Alicia was without the daily stress of her financial predicament, she quickly forgot all about the car she had once coveted.

Let them eat steel.

—THE BATTLE CRY OF BANKRUPTCY LAWYERS
RETURNING CLIENTS' CARS TO CREDITORS —

When you purchase something that you must make payments on, whether it's a house, a car, a furniture set or an expensive electronic device, you are in possession of it as long as you can make the payments each and every month until it is paid for. Until then, however, the "thing" you are paying on every month actually owns you.

When you go off to work every morning, you are doing it to earn what you need to live. But you are also doing it because you have to pay for the things you belong to. You are working for the house that has lost a lot of value recently. You are working for the vacation you took a year ago but are still paying for. You are working for all the things you financed to fill the rooms of your house. You are working for the car whose novelty wore off after the fifth payment.

If your financial situation has reached a crisis point, you must take the remedy that will cure you. After meeting with a bankruptcy specialist, you may learn that you'll have to let go of certain things. Or you may learn that you will be able to keep everything you've acquired. Whether the antidote tastes bad or is very delicious, it's important for your healing process to take the medicine.

If you don't, you will not get well again.

FIVE THINGS TO DO IF YOU ARE <u>NOT</u> FILING BANKRUPTCY

- Get a second job or find a way to make money.

- Stop using credit and save for things in advance.

- Contact your credit card companies to negotiate a payoff figure, and find a way to pay it off with a second job. Remember, you may still have a negative credit rating impact for the write-off. You may also have to report the charge-off as income to the IRS.

- Carefully consider consumer credit counseling agencies. Not all of them are truly non-profit agencies that will improve your situation. Some charge large fees and withhold payment to your creditor, damaging your credit score further. Be wary and ask lots of questions.

- Prioritize debts for repayment, starting with highest-interest debts first.

FROM THE TRUTH TO THE CURE

- Are you more like Kevin who was willing to let go of his car in exchange for eliminating his debts, or more like Alicia who clung to her car until she couldn't stand the harassment any more? Remember, you may be able to keep your car, depending on how much property you own and where you live.

- Have you heard any of the common myths about bankruptcy?

- Do you understand some of the fundamental truths about bankruptcy?

- Do you believe that bankruptcy is good or bad?

THE THREE UNIVERSAL TRUTHS

1. Financial crisis has distinct emotional stages, *especially* denial.

2. Bankruptcy is designed to *help* honest people, not hurt them.

3. Those without knowledge are those without power. With the knowledge of the truth, you claim the power to resolve your financial crisis.

ARE YOU BANKRUPT?

Many of our clients are unaware when they come into our office that they are already bankrupt. While they have not legally filed for bankruptcy, their incoming cash flow doesn't meet their outgoing expenses. Their inability to pay debts as they come due is also known as insolvency. The IRS defines insolvency as having more total liabilities than the fair market value of your assets. However without a huge pile of savings or a trust fund, most people need cash flow to pay debts as they come due. Yet for some reason, it comes as a shock to most people that without cash flow sufficient to meet their expenses, they are living in a state of bankruptcy. For many, the only means of climbing out in the foreseeable future is availing themselves of the federally mandated regulations to forgive their debt—the Bankruptcy Code—the Main Street, USA bailout.

FROM THE TRUTH TO THE CURE

If you are seeking the truth, this is the place to start.

- Do you have cash flow?

- Look at your home value. Is it worth less than what you owe?

- Is the same true for your car?

- Is all the stuff you bought on your credit cards worth less than what you owe your credit card companies?

If you have no cash flow and your assets are not worth what you owe on them, you should see a bankruptcy lawyer who has specialized in this area of law to discuss your situation. If you have a plan to remedy the situation in 18–24 months, you may be able to avoid filing for bankruptcy. If not, the sooner you accept your truth, the sooner you can get to the cure with as much as possible to rebuild your financial future.

> *When you know better, you do better.*
>
> — Maya Angelou, often quoted by Oprah Winfrey —

BUT I HAVE AN IRA AND EQUITY IN MY HOUSE

This is where most people go wrong. Since Congress intended you to keep certain assets, otherwise known as *exempt assets,* don't consider them to be "money in the bank" available to use to pay those debts. These are the financial tools Congress intended you to keep to ensure your fresh start, to keep you from being a drain on the taxpayers down the road.

Exempt assets vary from state to state so you need to seek the advice of an attorney where you live to see what applies to you. For example, if your monthly income doesn't pay your bills but you have money in an IRA, don't look to your IRA as a short-term solution to your problems. If you have money in an annuity or home equity, don't think of those assets as emergency funds. If you do, you will be like the clients coming into our office who liquidated those assets and gave the proceeds away to their creditors before filing bankruptcy. You are intended to keep the financial tools you need to rebuild your future. Please do not make this common mistake.

Now you know better.

THE ANATOMY OF A BANKRUPTCY

When you are about to have a medical procedure, you may receive written instructions to follow in the days prior to the procedure. They may say not to smoke, take blood thinners, or eat or drink anything for a certain number of hours beforehand.

Let's face it. There's always somebody in the crowd who thinks he knows better than the expert. The rules don't apply to him. They are nothing more than broad guidelines to be stretched. We all know someone like that. You tell him not to smoke before his procedure, and he sneaks a cigarette on the way to the hospital. What difference does a little sip of water make prior to getting anesthesia? Well, it could be a life-threatening difference. When information like this is given to patients, it is to keep them from dying from a procedure designed to save their life, not end it.

The same is true for bankruptcy. It is designed to save people's financial lives, not end them. However if certain guidelines are not followed, failure to follow the rules can be lethal to your financial future.

Wrong is for other people.

— Fanny Brice (1891–1951) —

Take this scenario. Let's say you own lots of stuff like jewelry, a couple of cars that you own outright, and a valuable coin collection. There are a number of alternatives for someone like this filing bankruptcy who discloses the full truth to their bankruptcy lawyer.

Some people think, *Well, I'd rather give my car and coin collection to Aunt Tilly since they'll be taken away anyway.*

Well, that's not up to you. Making a transfer to keep goods out of the hands of the bankruptcy estate is fraudulent. You will lose your discharge, and you could go to jail.

Plus, poor Aunt Tilly would be in a heap of trouble.

As a matter of fact, this is the one exception to the rule that you should not represent yourself. If you are trying to shuffle your assets around in anticipation of filing bankruptcy, then by all means, represent yourself. I don't know a lawyer in his or her right mind anywhere who would want to represent you.

Now if you inadvertently made a boo-boo and did something like this, go to your bankruptcy lawyer and tell him. The Trustee in Bankruptcy is entitled to return of that property from the person who has it and will distribute the proceeds from a sale of that property to your creditors. Or there are other bankruptcy alternatives.

But whatever you do, disclose, disclose, disclose. That is the only way for the Court to distinguish the honest, but unfortunate debtor from the dishonest ones. If you made a mistake, disclosure and an honest attempt to right the wrong can make all the difference.

Failure to disclose equates to being sneaky and dishonest in the eyes of the Court. It will all go downhill from there. If you have a lawyer, he will likely file a motion to withdraw from your case.

When you were a kid, you learned the song, "The Farmer in the Dell." This situation would end much the same way; the cheese stands alone.

THINGS NOT TO DO

So here is a short (but not exhaustive) list of *things not to do:*

- Since my parents' home was put in my name just for estate-planning purposes, we'll just take my name off before I file for bankruptcy.

- Since the car is really for my daughter who is in college, we'll just put it in her name where it really belongs.

- We'll just fail to mention our matching Cartier watches and the jewelry we inherited from Grandma. No one will know the difference.

- We'll hide all of our valuable stuff at our buddy's house until the bankruptcy case is all over.

Any of these tactics are fraud—pure and simple. If you hide the truth, you will lose your discharge. You also could be prosecuted. Your lawyer will want nothing to do with you. Your buddy could also go to jail. Grandma will roll over in her grave.

Now let's say you already moved the title around on something for whatever reason, and now you know better. What should you do? Don't start switching everything around again without talking to legal counsel. Tell your bankruptcy lawyer. The situation can be properly disclosed and resolved. Remember, the truth will set you free. Isn't that a relief?

THE SHORT END OF THE STICK

Beware of the Short Sale

These days we hear a lot about short sales. They occur when the mortgage amount is greater than the current value of the property. To accomplish a short sale, the lender must agree to permit the sale at an amount less than the outstanding mortgage amount. So it's "short." Say you owe $200,000 on a piece of property that will only sell for $80,000 in today's market. You would have to obtain permission from the lender to forgive the unpaid balance in a short sale. The truth is many lenders have to file foreclosures rather than consent to short sales to obtain clear title to the property. However, even if you believe that your lender would permit a short sale, there are several reasons you should *not* do so if you are considering a bankruptcy.

One of the beautiful things about bankruptcy is that debt discharged in bankruptcy falls outside the tax consequences of forgiven debt under IRS guidelines.[6] So you don't have to pay Uncle Sam for the debt forgiven in bankruptcy.

A short sale is different. It may have tax consequences as forgiven debt, particularly if the property is not your primary residence. Doing a short sale right before filing a bankruptcy can result in owing Uncle Sam some money *not* dischargeable in bankruptcy, at least not right away. If you skip the short sale and file bankruptcy, you'll have no tax liability on the debt forgiven for the unpaid balance on the mortgage.

As of this writing, a law is in effect from 2007 through 2012 called The Mortgage Forgiveness Debt Relief Act of 2007. It excuses taxes on forgiven debt from a short sale of one's primary residence. Currently this does *not* apply to a second home or investment property, but the law could change. Even if you are *not* filing bankruptcy, you should consult an attorney and tax professional regarding the consequences of a short sale before doing it. You can also check the IRS Web site at www.irs.gov for more information on tax liability for cancellation of debt.

If you *are* considering bankruptcy, speak with a bankruptcy attorney in your state to determine how this impacts you if you are considering a short sale. For now, *do not do a short sale* without consulting with a bankruptcy attorney or tax professional first.

By the way, the recommendation to do a short sale from a real estate agent is *not* legal advice. A real estate agent stands to earn a commission from a short sale, and the agent may be completely unaware of the adverse tax consequences to you. It would be tragic to go through the hassle of showing your home, negotiating with a buyer, jumping through the voluminous hoops of obtaining a sale with your lender and then learning it cost you thousands, tens of thousands, or even hundreds of thousands of dollars *you never would have owed* had you left it all alone and just filed bankruptcy.

Now you know better.

WHAT IS NOT DISCHARGEABLE IN BANKRUPTCY

Chapter 7 and Chapter 13 are the typical bankruptcies for the consumer debtor.[7] The types of debts discharged vary, depending on the type of bankruptcy filed.

If you are a Chapter 13 debtor, certain types of debts are *not* discharged. They include, but are not limited to:[8]

- Mortgages owed outside the duration of the Chapter 13 Plan of Reorganization

- Spousal and child support

- Student loans that do not meet the legal standard for undue hardship

- Drunk-driving liabilities
- Willful and malicious injury that caused personal injury or death
- Criminal fines and restitution
- Fraud
- Other long-term obligations that fall outside the length of the plan.

If you file a Chapter 7, you will *not* discharge the following:[9]

- Alimony and child support
- Debts related to driving while intoxicated
- Fraud
- Debts determined non-dischargeable in a prior bankruptcy case due to fraud
- Student loans that cannot be demonstrated to meet the legal standard of undue hardship
- Local, state, and federal taxes incurred within a limited time frame
- Restitution, fines, and penalties imposed by the government
- Court fees
- Debts or creditors you fail to disclose on your bankruptcy petition

Creditors have the right to object to certain additional types of debt being discharged by filing a lawsuit against you in your bankruptcy case. If they can prove their case, they can keep additional types of debts from being discharged. These may include but are not limited to:[10]

- Certain luxury goods or services incurred within ninety days before the bankruptcy case is filed, including certain cash advances

- Debts incurred fraudulently

- Debts from willful and malicious acts

- Debts from embezzlement, larceny, or breach of fiduciary duty

DO I GET TO KEEP MY HOUSE?

Can you afford it? If you are behind on your payments, you and your lawyer will discuss whether you should keep your home. Even if you are current on your house, you should still have this discussion. There are many people who owe more on their homes right now than they are worth. This is your opportunity to decide which past financial decisions are ones you should stick with. It is also your chance to walk away from the bad deals and just keep the good ones.

Home is where the heart is.
—Gaius Plinius Secundas—Pliny the Elder—
(AD 23–August 24, AD 79), Como, Italy

Chapter 7 will not permit you to save your home from foreclosure if you are behind on payments. The lender will be able to obtain relief from the automatic stay from the Bankruptcy Court to resume the foreclosure process. This may slow things down a bit, but ultimately the home will go back to the lender.

Chapter 13 is a pretty slick alternative for those who are behind on payments, have a regular source of income and want to keep their home. Any arrearage on the home is paid through the plan in addition to the regular monthly payments.

Check with your bankruptcy attorney regarding the current state of the law with regard to Chapter 13. It is a wonderful alternative for those seeking to keep their homes and who can still afford them.

SHOULD I FILE BANKRUPTCY?

A reputable bankruptcy attorney will look at your individual facts and give you a recommendation. After speaking with the attorney, go home and think about it. Talk to your spouse.

The longer you wait to seek the help of a professional, however, the more likely you are to liquidate exempt assets. These assets are intended for you, not for your creditors. Don't allow your creditors to turn you over, shake you, and empty every last penny out of your pockets before filing bankruptcy.

Our government has very good reasons for wanting you to walk out of Bankruptcy Court with some assets still in your possession. It is in our collective best interest for each of us to have financial resources of our own to build our financial futures. That helps better ensure that we will not be a drain on taxpayers later.

FROM THE TRUTH TO THE CURE

- Would you be willing to give up certain assets you own to obtain forgiveness of debt although it might not be necessary to do so?

- Did you know that a short sale on property that isn't your primary residence could result in owing Uncle Sam taxes?

- Did you know that negotiating with creditors to settle debt outside bankruptcy can also result in owing Uncle Sam taxes?

- Did you know that filing bankruptcy will not result in owing any income taxes for the debts canceled inside the bankruptcy case?

- Have you considered how much money you would have available if your debts were forgiven in bankruptcy?

CHAPTER TEN

CHOOSING THE RIGHT MEDICINE

The only medicine for suffering, crime, and
all the other woes of mankind, is wisdom.

— THOMAS HUXLEY (1825 - 1895) —

KNOWLEDGE

At your disposal is the information you need to now make your decision. You have recognized the warning signs in your life, and now you know the truth—your truth. So what is the cure for you?

It is knowledge followed by action.

Finding the Right Lawyer

If you have any doubts about the right course, see a specialist who can advise you. Think of it as seeing a doctor, just as you would if you were afraid you were exhibiting symptoms of a serious illness. Medical doctors are M.D.'s.

Similarly, attorneys are J.D.'s, juris doctors, or doctors of law. Start gathering names. Talk to other people you know who have filed bankruptcy. Who did they use? Were they happy with the communication with their lawyer? Observe a Meeting of Creditors at your local Bankruptcy Court to see the attorneys who are doing a lot of the cases. Which one do you like? Ask for his or her card and call for an appointment. Release the shame and guilt. Be grateful for the knowledge that will allow you to have a fresh start and breathe in the air of living debt-free.

A rich man is nothing but a poor man with money.
— W.C. FIELDS —

Movers and Shakers and Millionaire Makers

If you want to get some idea of the kind of people who really file bankruptcy, check online for famous people who have filed bankruptcy. You will find several of the early Presidents of the United States, a Secretary of State, senators, governors, a Treasury Secretary (ironic, isn't it?), founders of major corporations, television interviewers, authors, founders of movie companies, lots of actors, and entertainers. Most are still recognized as accomplished individuals who made important contributions to our history.

These people found a new beginning following forgiveness of their debt. Perhaps it is fair to say that bankruptcy may have even given them a jump-start to their ultimate success.

That is the very idea behind bankruptcy. It is far better for us all if those who receive a discharge of their debts would excel in their new life with a fresh start. Consider how your life might be different if you could move forward debt-free.

Robert G. Allen's Story:
The Millionaire Maker—In His Own Words

Personal insight shared by Robert G. Allen,
New York Times bestselling author of *Nothing Down* and *Creating Wealth*

People know that I'm a *New York Times* bestselling author—a financial and real estate guru who knows how to make money, keep money and build a financial empire. What most people don't know is that I also know the other side of the story—the side so many people find themselves in now. One of the greatest challenges of my life came when the financial empire I had spent my life building crumbled beneath me. A few bad decisions met with catastrophe. Suddenly my life changed. Not only did I feel differently about myself, but I assumed everyone else felt differently about me too.

Once I thought I was untouchable because of impressive numbers on a balance sheet. They were like a coat of armor. But as those impressive numbers diminished to zero, then less than zero, so did my self-worth. I felt vulnerable and defeated. My relationships suffered.

How could I have failed my wife and family?

I dreaded going to the mailbox. Finally I came to grips with what I had to do, and I went to see a bankruptcy attorney. It was a day I dreaded, a day I will never forget, but I knew that it was the right thing to do. It was, shall we say . . . a *learning* experience.

What I learned was that my financial recovery required more than legal forgiveness of my debt. It required me to forgive myself—for mistakes I had made, for disappointing my family, for falling from the pedestal where I once felt admired. For awhile I thought bankruptcy had ruined my life.

But the truth is, bankruptcy saved it.

What ruined my life was an avalanche—an avalanche of bad decisions, denial and, well, a literal avalanche that wiped out my house and my dreams. The truth is that bankruptcy was the giant snow plow that moved the frozen mountain left by an avalanche. It legally forgave my debt. As the debt melted, so did the feeling of dread I'd felt while walking to the mailbox. I started to regain my old confidence. With no more interest accruing, penalties lifted, and an umbrella of protection surrounding me, I could once again feel the protection from even a higher source.

Forgiveness affected far more than my debts—it permeated my soul, my relationship with my wife, my friends, and my future. I had a second chance at my financial life and my relationships. This time I would build my financial empire with a foundation of strength, with the forgiveness that had been given to me and that I could share with others.

I had the chance to get to know Jo Anne Shumard during an infomercial shoot for one of my books. She reminded me of what I'd personally learned—how bankruptcy changes many lives for the better. You will find that this team has a rare combination of experience, wisdom and compassion, sprinkled with a little tough-love. Their backgrounds cover just about all the angles of attacking debt. They know the creditors' side, the court side and the consumer-advocacy side. They'll hold your hand, perhaps scold you, but in the end empower you to make the right decision for yourself—and for your family.

There is no blame here—no judgment. There is insight, wisdom, understanding . . . and some shocking truth.

There is a reason you picked up this book. Don't put it away until you have taken it all in. These are lawyers and friends who can help you find your truth.

All the best to you in your fresh start.

ACTION

Actions speak louder than words.

— 1736 MELANCHOLY STATE OF PROVINCE IN
A. M. DAVIS COLONIAL CURRENCY (1911) III. 137 —

Your First Appointment

Take action. Make an appointment with a bankruptcy attorney. Make a list of questions you are particularly concerned about so you are organized and ready to have your concerns addressed. Bankruptcy attorneys are swamped, and their time is valuable. Be prepared to pay a fee for the valuable service provided to you. You want the best attorney you can find who specializes in this area for it is with the help of this professional that you will obtain the knowledge you need to have a fresh start. It is the best investment you can make in your future.

By the way, this is not the time to hire a typing service, Internet service, paralegal service, or jack-of-all-trades. These people will never be able to provide you the guidance that an attorney with years of experience in a Bankruptcy Court can. A mistake made can cost you tens of thousands, if not hundreds of thousands of dollars in debts that could have been but were not discharged.

A man who represents himself has a fool for a client.

— ABRAHAM LINCOLN —

Start tracking your income and expenses now so you will have that information when you see your lawyer. Where is your money going? After all, why is there credit card debt if you really are living within your means? Ask the attorney what to bring to the appointment. For example, we don't want our clients to bring in a stack of bills. We need to know your income, your expenses, your payments on your house and car and what they're worth, and any lawsuits against you. Check with your attorney to see what they need.

Jeannie: Live, Learn and Teach a Friend

Jeannie was a client of ours several years ago. Like so many, she and her husband ran into financial problems soon after her husband was laid off. His unemployment benefits were enough to allow them to cover their basic living expenses, but little more. They were in trouble and needed help. After assessing their situation, we decided that filing for relief under Chapter 7 was their best option.

Their bankruptcy case wasn't anything out of the ordinary. We went to court where everything went smoothly. Jeannie and her husband surrendered an SUV that got terrible gas mileage and was worth less than half what they owed on it, discharging the entire debt on the vehicle. They also discharged over thirty-five thousand dollars of credit card debt they would have paid on for years and years. They didn't ask how bankruptcy would affect their credit; they didn't care. All they wanted to know was that the tens of thousands of dollars of debt they were struggling with every single day would be gone forever. It was.

About a year after their case was closed, Jeannie began referring people to our office who were in the same situation she had been in. This is a validation and a reward. It tells us that what we do makes enough of a difference in people's lives that they, in turn, want others they care about to receive the same help and relief.

Recently Jeannie came with one of her friends and sat in on our first meeting. She told us, as so many others have, that filing bankruptcy was one of the best decisions she'd ever made. Soon after her case was discharged, she received a credit card in the mail, which she is now using (carefully) to re-establish her credit. About six months after her case was discharged, she was able to refinance her house, consolidating two mortgages into one at a lower interest rate. The gas hog she surrendered was quickly replaced by another vehicle she can afford to drive. Most importantly, when she tried to finance something she didn't really need, the store was reluctant to extend her credit at first. Waiting for the credit manager's approval gave her time to think about what she was about to do and what she had already been through. Those few minutes of contemplation allowed her to realize she didn't really need what she was about to buy, so she got up and walked out of the store. I have heard Jeannie's story told again and again by new clients who were referred by old clients.

For some reason, people often worry that if they seek bankruptcy protection, they'll be "punished" by not being able to get credit again for many years. I remind them that credit has led them down the thorny and stressful path they are now traveling. Then I explain that soon after being pulled out from the deep hole they are trapped in, the credit industry will offer them a shiny new shovel with which to start digging a new hole. Your perpetual debt creates their perpetual profit.

FROM TRUTH TO THE CURE

- Do you believe, or have you heard from someone, that filing bankruptcy will "ruin" your credit? What if you knew that being debt-free actually makes you a safer credit risk?

- Do you believe, or has someone told you, that people who file bankruptcy are "deadbeats?" What if you knew that people who pay their credit card balances in full every month are actually named "deadbeats" by the banking industry because the banks make no profit from them?[11]

- Do you believe, or have you read somewhere, that you won't get credit for seven years if you file bankruptcy? What if you knew that most people who go through bankruptcy are able to successfully reestablish credit within a few *months* after their discharge?

The truth is that providing credit generates an enormous profit. When someone receives a discharge in bankruptcy, they are usually debt-free (with some exceptions), and they may not be able to get relief in bankruptcy again for anywhere from four to eight years depending on what type of case they filed. If you don't owe anyone money and you can't get bankruptcy relief for several years, you are a very safe credit risk, and you will be able to obtain credit again.

The following information is to help you get on track for your fresh start. Below are a few suggestions to get started on a cure designed especially for you.

CHAPTER ELEVEN

LIFE STRATEGIES

THE EASY WAY

You wanna do this the easy way, or the hard way . . .

THE DAILY CALENDAR

At your local drug store, you can find a very inexpensive pocket calendar. If you are married, buy one for your spouse. You will be using this only for keeping track of your daily expenses, not your appointments. Use a different kind of calendar for your appointments.

Keep it in your purse or car, wherever it will be closest to you and easiest to access. When you spend money or charge anything during the day, write it in the calendar that day, including the amount and what it was for. For example, "$5.50 latte at Moonstar's."

At the end of the day, when you are sitting in front of the TV, tally up your day's total. Every week tally up your weekly total. By looking at this every day, you will become more aware of that bag of candy you buy as a routine when you walk into the drug store or that magazine you pick up at the newsstand. Those are donations to an unworthy cause. You have better ways to spend that money. Start watching your bad habits disappear and your money reappearing.

Track your big expenses from your checkbook or online banking to see where you can cut back. Write out your expenses by name and the amount. Scrutinize every expense to see if you are duplicating services anywhere. Do you have duplicate long distance service at home and on your cell phone? Can you bundle your plan with Internet and cable? Do you need all those cell phone minutes? Do you really need or use your cell phone? Can you do better with a family plan or a prepaid plan?

We often wander aimlessly, giving away what's left in our wallets without even realizing how much we are spending. Pay attention, be proactive, and start with where you spend your money. It's well worth it.

BACK TO BASICS

Find a penny pick it up. It will bring you lots of luck.
Find a penny give it to a friend,
and your luck comes back again.

— CHILDHOOD RHYME —

NEGOTIATE EVERYTHING

The Pregnant Pause

Your life is comprised of one negotiation after another. You may not think you're an expert at this, but the truth is, you have lots of experience in negotiating. And everything is negotiable. It's best to come prepared to any negotiation with comparables for whatever product or service you are negotiating. If you don't like the response you receive to a negotiation, be silent. Silence is one of the most powerful tools in the world. Have you ever heard that the first one who speaks after an offer is made loses? That pregnant pause can be filled with money in your pocket. If the compromise is not suitable, be prepared to walk away.

GOOD AS GOLD

Water is Gold

When our water bill came, I noticed that the average use of water for irrigating a home in our area is 18,000 gallons per month. Yikes. Our use is zero. More than ten years ago, we noticed how much fertilizer and water it took to keep a lawn, so we hired a landscape architect to draw up a plan of drought-tolerant native plants that would thrive in our climate. We separated each plant and spread them out thinly across the yard, replacing the lawn one area at a time. Now we have a lush tropical garden full of flowers, fruits, and herbs that requires no irrigation.

If the idea of pouring thousands of gallons of water a month into your yard leaves your throat dry, it may be time to think differently about your yard. Maybe it *shouldn't* look like everybody else's. Water is a precious resource we need to treat like the gold that it is. Too many people lack it all over the world, and we need to conserve this precious resource just as we do natural gas, oil and electricity. Sure it will save money. More importantly, it will save the resource.

Gas is Gold

We learned that already, didn't we? If you're in a climate and community where it would be safe to travel on a motor scooter, give it some consideration. They get around eighty miles to the gallon and are an awful lot of fun. We saw so many families traveling in Italy on their scooters that we found ourselves falling in love with the convenience and fun of traveling this way. Give it some thought, save your gas money, and enjoy the ride.

Stripping Away the Electric Bills

So many of us have major electronics around the house—big TV's, DVD players, game systems, computers, chargers, you name it. Those that aren't on power strips to protect from electric surges should be. Once they are on them, consider unplugging the strips when they are not in use and plugging them in only when you need them. Many devices run constantly and eat away at your electric bill even when you aren't using them. Give unplugging a try and watch your electric bill decrease.

KNOW "NO"

It's fair to say that we see things differently and do things differently without a lot of concern about what our friends might be doing. They have often asked our "trick" for raising kids who do so well in school. First we acknowledge their God-given gifts and drive. Aside from that, we did take an unconventional approach.

Our first child was raised with no cable television. As a matter of fact, at first there was no television at all. We never had cable until two years ago. We also didn't purchase video games for the kids as they grew up. We wanted the kids to play outside, read books, and talk to us. We finally relented to a video gaming system when an uncle was unloading an old one at a garage sale with a box of games. By then, the boys were fairly grown up. They had already watched some of their friends become addicted to video games, rarely leaving the house to engage in any activity unless it involved staring at a screen.

We attribute the lack of exposure to video games and cable TV as key elements in our kids' academic success. Once they were older and saved up their own money, they were allowed to make the decision to buy their own TV and video game system. They had to make the decision to take their limited resources and devote them to that "want." Living with that decision is a lesson in itself.

We believe those precious early years of knowing "no" may have made all the difference in giving them both an academic head start.

The real key is thinking for your own family without regard to what other families may be doing. What seems acceptable to everyone else might not be the right thing to do for your family.

I want my children to have all the things I couldn't afford. Then I want to move in with them.

— PHYLLIS DILLER —

IS YOUR STUFF KILLING YOU?

So many of us have loaded our homes beyond capacity. It seems that being a homeowner leads to the acquisition stage of life—furniture, accessories, yard decorations, and more furniture for the outdoors, lawn equipment, holiday decorations. Before we know it, we need a storage facility.

How ridiculous is it that we own so much, we can't fit it in our house any more? We lose track of what we have and purchase duplicate items because we can't get to the thing we know we own, but just can't find.

Simplicity is the answer. Clean it out and get it in the hands of someone who actually needs it, someone who will use it, appreciate it, and wear it out before it crumbles to the ground unused. Even better is getting items that you need or want in return for stuff you're ready to get rid of.

THE SWAP MEET

A few years back, we had one heck of a hurricane season in Florida. We were hit with one after the other and could barely leave our home. Fallen trees blocked the streets and debris was everywhere. Trucks had trouble delivering necessary goods and services. Even the post office couldn't deliver mail. We had no power for quite awhile. The one thing we learned was that among the neighbors, we had virtually everything we needed. One neighbor hooked us into his generator. We had a freezer full of food that we shared before it thawed and spoiled. Another had a lot of rakes and power tools we all used to clean out one another's yards.

These economic times take me back to those wonderful memories of the neighborhood working together to make sure we all had what we needed to get through the storm. Did I say wonderful? You bet. Those were some great memories.

My point is that if we actually spoke to our neighbors on a more regular basis, we might be surprised to find out just how capable we are of helping one another with what we need. I truly believe that we will have to start thinking and acting differently to flourish in this economic climate. Those who reach out to their friends and neighbors will flourish. Those who hold tight in their own little universe won't have the resources they need.

But it must be cooperative—everybody must be willing to do his or her share to make this work.

How about a Saturday swap meet at a cul-de-sac in your neighborhood? Everybody brings what they don't need anymore. If you bring an item to swap, you can take an item you need. What isn't swapped can be sold or sent to charity. We could clean out our closets and help each other while having fun. Different swap meets could have themes: The Diva Designer Exchange (labels only, ladies); Handyman Hardware Swap; The Kiddie Carnival (bikes and baby equipment). Use your imagination and watch how little you will ever need to buy.

ENTERTAINING

Pot Luck

Going out means going broke. Remember the days of playing records in the basement with a cooler full of your favorite drinks? Okay, so we're older than you are. Our point is to start inviting people over to our homes for potluck meals and our favorite tunes. Theme parties are so much fun—the '70s, pirates, Las Vegas.

Pot luck means everybody has to bring something to help out. Let go. Who cares if there are duplicate dishes? Get out those favorite CD's and have some laughs. Nobody expects anything fancy here. This is about fun and friendship without busting the bank. And while you've got everybody together, plan your next swap meet.

Hors d'oeuvre: A ham sandwich cut into forty pieces.

— JACK BENNY —

THE VICTORY GARDEN

My parents used to tell about some land they were allowed to use to garden during World War II when it was hard to get fresh produce. Perhaps you know someone who would allow you to garden on their property. Or perhaps you are the one who would allow others to use your property to garden. In exchange, they could let you have some produce. Years ago I started planting many things in my yard that were edible.

In Florida we have ginger, bananas, oranges, and lemons. We've grown strawberries, potatoes, zucchini, cucumbers, peppers, basil, fennel, avocado, pineapple and tomatoes. My mouth waters just thinking about it. Planting a garden with your kids teaches them a lot about life and reaping the rewards of honest labor.

FINDING YOUR CURE

- Have you learned anything that empowers you to take action to resolve your financial problems?

- What ideas can you implement to get your fresh start?

- What action can you take now to get started?
- Do you have a calendar you can use to track your daily expenses?
- Do you track your monthly expenses online or through your checkbook?
- How can you save water?
- Do you know what plants are drought-tolerant for your climate?
- Would you enjoy owning a scooter?
- When was the last time you said "no" to your kids?
- Are video games and cable TV a good influence on your children?
- Could you save money by having pot luck dinners rather than going out?
- Do you have a place for a garden, or do you know someone who would let you garden on their property?

CHAPTER TWELVE

NO SHAME

Over thirty years ago, Congress enacted the Bankruptcy Code providing relief to the honest but unfortunate debtor. Congress intended to help out the good people who found themselves in bad situations. It is, in essence, the Main Street, USA bailout. It was not intended to shame anyone anymore than an honest taxpayer should feel guilt or shame for taking a tax deduction that is lawful and honest.

It's interesting that as the bankruptcy laws evolved to help good people in trouble, so too did a resounding chorus in the media that, "Bankruptcy should be your last resort. It will ruin your life. It will destroy your credit."

Let's not forget that many of the "experts" in the media began as stock brokers and financial planners. Many of these brilliant and intelligent people gave sound advice to their loyal viewers and listeners. As the economy deteriorated, they found themselves talking about bankruptcy. Many of these folks don't have bankruptcy experience. They haven't been trained in the field and don't know much about it at all.

A billion here, a billion there, and pretty soon
you're talking about real money.

— Robert Frost (1879–1963) —

There were also other "experts" involved in the same industries that happened to be receiving a government bailout, an industry that is reported to have spent $77 million dollars last year lobbying our government representatives and $37 million in federal campaign contributions for a bailout that may now exceed a trillion dollars. With the paltry payout as of February 4, 2009 of a mere $295.2 billion (only one third of the total), this would be a return of 258,449 percent.[12] Shame is a fascinating concept, isn't it?

The government who robs Peter to pay Paul
can always depend on the support of Paul.

— George Bernard Shaw —

There should be no shame for those of you who find yourselves in unfortunate circumstances. The shame is with an industry that stacked the deck against you. It's an industry that constantly changes the rules; that could change your credit card rates and terms for any reason at any time; an industry that makes money off penalties and default interest rates that would be illegal, violating usury laws, between average citizens; an industry that is still pillaging the public by taking taxpayer dollars and squandering them on luxurious trips, jets and office renovations while you're scraping by and can't pay your mortgage.

Indeed, there is no shame. The shame should be with the industry, not you.

We see good people every day who punish themselves with guilt and shame, who think they are bad because of the situation they find themselves in. It's as though a terrorist released a bacteria into our society, and those who are sick are blaming themselves for bad hygiene. It really isn't your fault.

Sure you've been kept in the dark. Apparently some of our friends and government representatives are still lost in the haze. The problem with the industry is so insidious that it's not going to be easy to change things around. We know there are no easy solutions to fix this globally, that's for sure. But there are simple remedies for individuals and families. That is where we must begin.

First, look into your wallet. Then look into your heart. Look at your family and know that there is never any shame in doing the right thing for them. There are warning signs, there is truth, and there is a cure. We hope we've given you the tools you need to take the first step.

We are here to listen.

We want to know how you feel having taken this journey with us. If you agree that no honest person should feel shame for being in unfortunate circumstances, please let us know. Send us an email at authors@isyourwalletkillingyou.com.

We will also have special offers for readers who leave us their contact information. You will have access to new information, newsletters, and upcoming books at special discounts. Use the discount code "CPR" when prompted.

If you think the banking and credit industries should be the ones who are ashamed, tell us that too. We want to hear from you and share that resounding voice with the media and our government representatives.

The banks have throngs of people lobbying for them. Now you have a voice. Use it. We're listening. If your wallet is killing you, get Financial CPR. We've shown you how.

Thanks on behalf of all of us who will benefit from your courageous first step. When you can put your debt behind you and become a productive member of society, without the noose of debt around your neck, you contribute to us all with your joy, your presence, your work, and your tax dollars. Each breath of your new life breathes new life into this economy.

Congratulations, for you are well on your way to your fresh start. All the best in your new and prosperous life.

GLOSSARY OF BANKRUPTCY TERMINOLOGY

The US Courts Web site provides this information as well as other Bankruptcy related resources:

http://www.uscourts.gov/bankruptcycourts/
bankruptcybasics/glossary.html

341 meeting - The Meeting of Creditors required by section 341 of the Bankruptcy Code at which the debtor is questioned under oath by creditors, a trustee, examiner, or the US trustee about his/her financial affairs; also called creditors' meeting.

— A —

adversary proceeding - A lawsuit arising in or related to a bankruptcy case commenced by filing a complaint with the court.

assume - An agreement to continue performing duties under a contract or lease.

automatic stay - An injunction that automatically stops lawsuits, foreclosures, garnishments, and all collection activity against the debtor the moment a bankruptcy petition is filed.

— **B** —

bankruptcy - A legal procedure for dealing with debt problems of individuals and businesses; specifically a case filed under one of the Chapters of Title 11 of the United States Code (the Bankruptcy Code).

bankruptcy administrator - An officer of the judiciary serving in the judicial districts of Alabama and North Carolina who, like the US trustee, is responsible for supervising the administration of bankruptcy cases, estates, and trustees; monitoring plans and disclosure statements; monitoring creditors' committees; monitoring fee applications; and performing other statutory duties. Compare US Trustee.

Bankruptcy Code - The informal name for Title 11 of the United States Code (11 U.S.C. §§ 101-1330), the federal bankruptcy law.

Bankruptcy Court - The Bankruptcy Judges in regular active service in each district; a unit of the district court.

bankruptcy estate - All legal or equitable interests of the debtor in property at the time of the bankruptcy filing. The estate includes all property in which the debtor has an interest, even if it is owned or held by another person.

Bankruptcy Judge - A judicial officer of the United States District Court who is the court official with decision-making power over federal bankruptcy cases.

bankruptcy petition - The document filed by the debtor (in a voluntary case) or by creditors (in an involuntary case) by which opens the bankruptcy case. There are official forms for bankruptcy petitions.

— C —

Chapter 7 - The Chapter of the Bankruptcy Code providing for "liquidation," *i.e.*, the sale of a debtor's nonexempt property and the distribution of the proceeds to creditors.

Chapter 9 - The Chapter of the Bankruptcy Code providing for reorganization of municipalities, which includes cities and towns, as well as villages, counties, taxing districts, municipal utilities, and school districts.

Chapter 11 - The Chapter of the Bankruptcy Code providing (generally) for reorganization, usually involving a corporation or partnership. A Chapter 11 debtor usually proposes a plan of reorganization to keep its business alive and pay creditors over time. People in business or individuals can also seek relief in Chapter 11.

Chapter 12 - The Chapter of the Bankruptcy Code providing for adjustment of debts of a "family farmer" or a "family fisherman" as those terms are defined in the Bankruptcy Code.

Chapter 13 - The Chapter of the Bankruptcy Code providing for adjustment of debts of an individual with regular income. Chapter 13 allows a debtor to keep property and pay debts over time, usually three to five years.

Chapter 15 - The Chapter of the Bankruptcy Code dealing with cases of cross-border insolvency.

claim - A creditor's assertion of a right to payment from the debtor or the debtor's property.

confirmation - Bankruptcy Judges' approval of a plan of reorganization or liquidation in Chapter 11 or payment plan in Chapter 12 or 13.

consumer debtor - A debtor whose debts are primarily consumer debts.

consumer debts - Debts incurred for personal, as opposed to business, needs.

contested matter - Those matters, other than objections to claims, that are disputed but are not within the definition of adversary proceeding contained in Rule 7001.

contingent claim - A claim that may be owed by the debtor under certain circumstances, *e.g.,* where the debtor is a cosigner on another person's loan, and that person fails to pay.

creditor - One to whom the debtor owes money or one who claims to be owed money by the debtor.

credit counseling - Generally refers to two events in individual bankruptcy cases: (1) the "individual or group briefing" from a nonprofit budget and credit-counseling agency that individual debtors must attend prior to filing under any Chapter of the Bankruptcy Code, and (2) the "instructional course in personal financial management" in Chapters 7 and 13 that an individual debtor must complete before a discharge is entered. There are exceptions to both requirements for certain categories of debtors, exigent circumstances, or if the US trustee or bankruptcy administrator has determined that there are insufficient approved credit-counseling agencies available to provide the necessary counseling.

creditors' meeting - See 341 meeting.

current monthly income - The average monthly income received by the debtor over the six calendar months before commencement of the bankruptcy case, including regular contributions to household expenses from non-debtors and income from the debtor's spouse if the petition is a joint petition, but not including social-security income and certain other payments made because the debtor is the victim of certain crimes. 11 U.S.C. § 101(10A).

— D —

debtor - A person who has filed a petition for relief under the Bankruptcy Code.

debtor education - See credit counseling.

defendant - An individual or business against whom a lawsuit is filed.

discharge - A release of a debtor from personal liability for certain dischargeable debts set forth in the Bankruptcy Code. A discharge releases a debtor from personal liability for certain debts known as *dischargeable debts* (see below) and prevents the creditors owed those debts from taking any action against the debtor to collect the debts. The discharge also prohibits creditors from communicating with the debtor regarding the debt, including telephone calls, letters, and personal contact.

dischargeable debt - A debt for which the Bankruptcy Code allows the debtor's personal liability to be eliminated.

disclosure statement - A written document prepared by the Chapter 11 debtor or other plan proponent that is designed to provide "adequate information" to creditors to enable them to evaluate the Chapter 11 plan of reorganization.

— E —

equity - The value of a debtor's interest in property that remains after liens and other creditors' interests are considered. Example: If a house valued at $100,000 is subject to a $80,000 mortgage, there is $20,000 of equity.

executory contract or lease - Generally includes contracts or leases under which both parties to the agreement have duties remaining to be performed. If a contract or lease is executory, a debtor may assume it or reject it.

exemptions/exempt property - Certain property owned by an individual debtor that the Bankruptcy Code or applicable state law permits the debtor to keep from unsecured creditors. For example, in some states the debtor may be able to exempt all or a portion of the equity in the debtor's primary residence (homestead exemption), or some or all "tools of the trade" used by the debtor to make a living (*i.e.*, auto tools for an auto mechanic or dental tools for a dentist). The availability and amount of property the debtor may exempt depends on the state the debtor lives in.

— F —

family farmer/family fisherman - An individual, individual and spouse, corporation, or partnership engaged in a farming or fishing operation that meets certain debt limits and other statutory criteria for filing a petition under Chapter 12.

fraudulent transfer - A transfer of a debtor's property made with intent to defraud or for which the debtor receives less than the transferred property's value.

fresh start - The characterization of a debtor's status after bankruptcy, *i.e.,* free of most debts. Giving debtors a fresh start is one purpose of the Bankruptcy Code.

— I —

insider (of individual debtor) - Any relative of the debtor or of a general partner of the debtor; partnership in which the debtor is a general partner; general partner of the debtor; or a corporation of which the debtor is a director, officer, or person in control.

insider (of corporate debtor) - A director, officer, or person in control of the debtor; a partnership in which the debtor is a general partner; a general partner of the debtor; or a relative of a general partner, director, officer, or person in control of the debtor.

— J —

joint administration - A court-approved mechanism under which two or more cases can be administered together. Assuming no conflicts of interest, these separate businesses or individuals can pool their resources, hire the same professionals, etc.

joint petition - One bankruptcy petition filed by a husband and wife together.

— L —

lien - The right to take and hold or sell the property of a debtor as security or payment for a debt or duty.

liquidation - A sale of a debtor's property with the proceeds to be used for the benefit of creditors.

liquidated claim - A creditor's claim for a fixed amount of money.

— M —

means test - Applied by Section 707(b)(2) of the Bankruptcy Code, determines whether an individual debtor's Chapter 7 filing is presumed to be an abuse of the Bankruptcy Code requiring dismissal or conversion of the case (generally to Chapter 13). Abuse is presumed if the debtor's aggregate current monthly income (see definition above) over five years, net of certain statutorily allowed expenses is more than (i) $10,950, or (ii) 25% of the debtor's non-priority unsecured debt as long as that amount is at least $6,575. The debtor may rebut a presumption of abuse only by a showing of special circumstances that justify additional expenses or adjustments of current monthly income.

motion to lift the automatic stay - A request by a creditor to allow the creditor to take action against the debtor or the debtor's property that would otherwise be prohibited by the automatic stay.

— N —

no-asset case - A Chapter 7 case where there are no assets available to satisfy any portion of the creditors' unsecured claims.

non-dischargeable debt - A debt that cannot be eliminated in bankruptcy. Examples include a home mortgage, debts for alimony or child support, certain taxes, debts for most government funded or guaranteed educational loans or benefit overpayments, debts arising from death or personal injury caused by driving while intoxicated or under the influence of drugs, and debts for restitution or a criminal fine included in a sentence on the debtor's conviction of a crime. Some debts, such as debts for money or property obtained by false pretenses and debts for fraud or defalcation while acting in a fiduciary capacity, may be declared non-dischargeable only if a creditor timely files and prevails in a non-dischargeability action.

— O —

objection to dischargeability - A trustee's or creditor's objection to the debtor being released from personal liability for certain dischargeable debts. Common reasons include allegations that the debt to be discharged was incurred by false pretenses or that debt arose because of the debtor's fraud while acting as a fiduciary.

objection to exemptions - A trustee's or creditor's objection to the debtor's attempt to claim certain property as exempt from liquidation by the trustee to creditors.

— P —

party in interest - A party who has standing to be heard by the court in a matter to be decided in the bankruptcy case. For most matters, the debtor, the US trustee, or bankruptcy administrator, the case trustee and creditors are *parties in interest.*

petition preparer - A business not authorized to practice law that prepares bankruptcy petitions.

plan - A debtor's detailed description of how the debtor proposes to pay creditors' claims over a fixed period of time.

plaintiff - A person or business that files a formal complaint with the court.

postpetition transfer - A transfer of the debtor's property made after the commencement of the case.

preference or preferential debt payment - A debt payment made to a creditor in the ninety day period before a debtor files bankruptcy (or within one year, if the creditor was an insider) that gives the creditor more than the creditor would receive in the debtor's Chapter 7 case.

presumption of abuse - See means test

priority - The Bankruptcy Code's statutory ranking of unsecured claims that determines the order in which unsecured claims will be paid if there is not enough money to pay all unsecured claims in full. For example, under the Bankruptcy Code's priority scheme, money owed to the case trustee or for prepetition alimony and/or child support must be paid in full before any general unsecured debt (*i.e.* trade debt or credit card debt) is paid.

priority claim - An unsecured claim that is entitled to be paid ahead of other unsecured claims not entitled to priority status. *Priority* refers to the order in which these unsecured claims are to be paid.

proof of claim - A written statement and verifying documentation filed by a creditor that describes the reason the debtor owes the creditor money. There is an official form for this purpose.

property of the estate - All legal or equitable interests of the debtor in property as of the commencement of the case.

— R —

reaffirmation agreement - An agreement by a Chapter 7 debtor to continue paying a dischargeable debt (such as an auto loan) after the bankruptcy, usually for the purpose of keeping collateral (*e.g.* a car) that would otherwise be subject to repossession.

— S —

schedules - Detailed lists filed by the debtor along with (or shortly after filing) the petition showing the debtor's assets, liabilities, and other financial information. Debtor must use official forms.

secured creditor - A creditor holding a claim against the debtor who has the right to take and hold or sell certain property of the debtor in satisfaction of some or all of the claim.

secured debt - Debt backed by a mortgage, pledge of collateral, or other lien; debt for which the creditor has the right to pursue specific pledged property upon default. Examples include home mortgages, auto loans and tax liens.

small business case - A special type of Chapter 11 case in which there is no creditors' committee (or where the creditors' committee is deemed inactive by the court) and in which the debtor is subject to more oversight by the US trustee than other Chapter 11 debtors.

The Bankruptcy Code contains certain provisions designed to reduce the time a small business debtor is in bankruptcy.

statement of financial affairs - A series of questions on an official form that the debtor must answer in writing concerning sources of income, transfers of property, lawsuits by creditors, etc.

statement of intention - A declaration made by a Chapter 7 debtor concerning plans for dealing with consumer debts that are secured by property of the estate.

substantive consolidation - Putting the assets and liabilities of two or more related debtors into a single pool to pay creditors. Courts are reluctant to allow substantive consolidation since the action must not only justify the benefit that one set of creditors receives, but also the harm that other creditors suffer as a result.

— T —

transfer - Any mode or means by which a debtor disposes of or parts with his/her property.

trustee - The representative of the bankruptcy estate who exercises statutory powers, principally for the benefit of the unsecured creditors, under the general supervision of the court and the direct supervision of the US Trustee or bankruptcy administrator. The trustee is a private individual or corporation appointed in all Chapter 7, Chapter 12, and Chapter 13 cases and some Chapter 11 cases. The trustee's responsibilities include reviewing the debtor's petition and schedules and bringing actions against creditors or the debtor to recover property of the bankruptcy estate. In Chapter 7 the trustee liquidates property of the estate and makes distributions to creditors. Trustees in Chapter 12 and 13 have similar duties to a Chapter 7 trustee and the additional responsibilities of overseeing the debtor's plan, receiving payments from debtors, and disbursing plan payments to creditors.

— U —

US Trustee - An officer of the Justice Department responsible for supervising the administration of bankruptcy cases, estates, and trustees; monitoring plans and disclosure statements; monitoring creditors' committees; monitoring fee applications; and performing other statutory duties. Compare *bankruptcy administrator.*

undersecured claim - A debt secured by property that is worth less than the full amount of the debt.

unliquidated claim - A claim for which a specific value has not been determined.

unscheduled debt - A debt that should have been listed by the debtor.

unsecured claim - A claim or debt for which a creditor holds no special assurance of payment, such as a mortgage or lien; a debt for which credit was extended based solely upon the creditor's assessment of the debtor's future ability to pay.

— V —

Voluntary transfer - A transfer of a debtor's property with the debtor's consent.

CITED SOURCES

Current online as of April 10, 2009

1. In the last half-century, researchers studying human behavior have identi-fied a variety of steps designed to guide us through life's challenges including addiction, grief and loss. From the familiar twelve-step program identified in the 1939 book, *Alcoholics Anonymous: The Story of How More Than One Hundred Men Have Recovered From Alcoholism,* to the five stages of grief identified by Elisabeth Kübler-Ross in *On Death and Dying,* these ideas were later attributed to many types of plights, including financial crisis. They dif-fer in many respects to our observations, but may be of interest to you should you wish to do further reading on this subject.

2. 15 U.S.C. Section 1692

3. www.pbs.org/kcts/affluenza; Affluenza: The All-Consuming Epidemic, John de Graaf, David Wann & Thomas H. Naylor, ISBN 1-57675-199-6; James, Oliver (2007). Affluenza: How to Be Successful and Stay Sane. Vermilion. ISBN 9780091900113; James, Oliver (2008). The Selfish Capitalist. Vermil-ion. ISBN 9780091923815; Affluenza: when too much is never enough, Clive Hamilton and Richard Dennis, Allen & Unwin 2005, ISBN 1-74114-671-2

4. www.calculatorweb.com

5. the "purpose of the Bankruptcy Act to [distribute] the assets of the bankrupt . . . among creditors and then to relieve the honest debtor from the weight of oppressive indebtedness and permit him to start afresh free from the ob-ligations and responsibilities consequent upon business misfortunes." Wil-liams v. United States. Fidelity & Guarantee Co., 236 U.S. 549, 554-55 (1915); Adeeb, 787 F.2d at 1345. This purpose affords the "honest but unfortunate debtor who surrenders for distribution the property which he owns at the time of bankruptcy, a new opportunity in life and a clear field for future ef-fort, unhampered by the pressure and discouragement of preexisting debt." Local Loan Co. v. Hunt, 292 U.S. 234, 244 (1934).

6. 11 U.S.C. Section 346(j); 26 U.S.C. Section 108

7. Although if you have substantial debt, you may find yourself in a Chapter 11.

8. 11 U.S.C. Section 1328

9. 11 U.S.C. Section 523

10. Id.

11. http://www.pbs.org/wgbh/pages/frontline/shows/credit/interviews/warren.

12. www.opensecrets.org/news/2009/02/tarp-recipients-paid-out-114-m.html

ABOUT THE AUTHORS

Husband and wife/attorney team Stuart Ferderer, J.D. and Jo Anne Shumard, J.D. have a powerful combination of experience in Bankruptcy Law. They are partners in the Bankruptcy Law Firm of Ferderer & Shumard, P.A. in Orlando, Florida where Stuart's background in debtors' rights is merged with Jo Anne's creditors' rights and experience working with the Bankruptcy Court Judiciary.

Each has over twenty years of experience in this field, allowing them to help clients in financial distress. Together they have been involved in thousands of bankruptcy cases for individuals and businesses throughout the state of Florida. Clients have come from all walks of life: doctors, garbage collectors, college students, lawyers, seniors on Social Security, postal carriers, and radio personalities—people like you.

Jo Anne and Stuart live in Winter Park, Florida where they have raised their family.

PLEASE SEND E-MAIL CORRESPONDENCE TO

authors@isyourwalletkillingyou.com

PLEASE SEND MAIL TO

Authors, Ferderer & Shumard, P.A.

PO Box 532057

Orlando, FL 32853-2057